The Saber-Tooth Curriculum

Harold Raymond Wayne Benjamin
(1893–1969)

The Saber-Tooth Curriculum

By J. Abner Peddiwell

(Harold R. W. Benjamin, 1893–1969)

Memorial Edition

McGraw-Hill Book Company

New York	St. Louis	San Francisco
Düsseldorf	Johannesburg	Kuala Lumpur
London	Mexico	Montreal
New Delhi	Panama	Rio de Janeiro
Singapore	Sydney	Toronto

Library of Congress Cataloging in Publication Data

Benjamin, Harold Raymond Wayne, 1893–1969.
    Saber-tooth curriculum.

    Bibliography: p.
    1. Education—Anecdotes, facetiae, satire, etc.
I. Title.
LA23.B43   1972   370'.2'07   72-1431
ISBN 0-07-049152-6

1234567890KPKP798765432

This book was set in Caledonia by Textbook Services, Inc. It was edited by
John Hendry and Marie Longyear. The designer was John Horton. Sally
Ellyson supervised production.

The printer and binder was The Book Press.

Contents

Introduction
  R. Lee Hornbake   *1*

The Saber-Tooth Curriculum
  J. Abner Peddiwell   *18*

A Historical Note on This Book and Its Author
  Curtis G. Benjamin   *171*

Under His Own Command: The Careers of Harold R. W. Benjamin
  Franklin Parker   *181*

A Bibliography
  Compiled by Franklin Parker   *187*

Committees for the Harold R. W.
  Benjamin National Memorial Fund   *199*

Introduction

The Saber-Tooth Curriculum was written in the summer of 1938 on the campus of a Rocky Mountain university. The book took the form of a series of apparently ludicrous lectures on Stone Age education, but in reality it was the profound reflection of one of America's best educational minds. Harold R. W. Benjamin was sensitive to the shortcomings of the prevailing educational theory and practice, he felt the demoralizing and debilitating impact of the economic depression, and he foresaw the imminence of an international holocaust whose outcome would be uncertain. More importantly, Benjamin understood the relationships among these phenomena, and he was distressed by the wide discrepancy between a society in disrepair and what it might have been through better education. Despite the intentional levity by way of a "classroom with the longest bar in the world," there is behind this architectural façade a deep-seated concern and a fair measure of concealed anger as well.

Although man has harnessed the energy of the atom and has walked on the moon since the book was written, *The Saber-Tooth Curriculum* is still timely. Many of the problems and human concerns which prevailed in the 1930s are still with us, and we still suffer from educational lag or educational misalignment. Benjamin held to the theory that as long as a society fails to bring its educational efforts — all of its behavior-changing ways — into focus with its goals and purposes, that society postpones its golden age. And, if the discrepancy becomes too great or too prolonged, a society will destroy itself.

Essentially *The Saber-Tooth Curriculum* cites the cultural origins of education; it relates the education of an individual to his social responsibilities; it reveals the potential misuse of instructional technique as a means of escape from the main educational issues; it explains how certain disciplines become academically sanctified; it examines the impact of technological innovations on employment; it highlights the plight of youth in a disheveled society. This is a comprehensive claim for such a short book, but it is all there.

There is no point in trying to recapitulate Harold Benjamin's tale beyond this brief statement of scope. *The Saber-Tooth Curriculum* is, of course, reprinted in full in this memorial edition. But there is something to be gained by reviewing the setting in which the story emerged and by inferring some of its present-day implications.

Harold Benjamin spent his early life on the open spaces of the

Northwest Frontier. Either by chance or by design Benjamin's education was on a stop-and-go-basis, and much was gained outside the classroom. Benjamin was a school principal before he participated in a border campaign touched off by the Mexican bandit Pancho Villa; he had seen combat in World War I before he completed his baccalaureate degree. He earned a living in a variety of occupations before earning his doctorate at Stanford University. Benjamin was attuned to the many signals that were communicating the important educational developments of the day, and he interpreted them well. Some of the signals were national, some international; some originated within the prevailing learning theory, some within educational practice. Benjamin's alias, J. Abner Peddiwell, while under the influence of personality-expanding tequila daisies, was able to make a single pattern of the dominant events of the day.

The National Scene

The United States had emerged from World War I as an international power, but we were uneasy in the role and not sure how to play it. We were not willing to formally accept internationalism by way of the League of Nations, but instead preferred an aloofness dependent upon the apparent security of two broad oceans buttressed by peace pacts and arms limitations. The domestic economic readjustment following World War I initially took the classical form of a short business recession followed by an expanding economy. The expansion lasted until 1929, when the economic bubble burst. Only then did our society as a whole admit uncertainty about some of the previously accepted economic axioms and uncertainty about the nation's goals as well.

When the crash bottomed out in the United States in 1933, 13 million persons were unemployed, and very few of the other 39 million in the work force were fully employed. The gross national product in 1933 was 55.7 billion dollars – approximately the dollar value of the goods imported into the United States in 1969 and a little less than was spent in 1969 for user-operated transportation (cars, gasoline, tires, repairs). As late as 1936, 78 out of every 100 persons earned or were in families that earned $2,000 a year, despite major efforts to create employment and to restore confidence.

Abroad, authoritarian governments had filled the political voids left in the wake of World War I – the war that was to "make the world safe for democracy." Russia became a totalitarian communist state; Italy, Germany, and Japan became fascist. Since an authoritarian state cannot abide idleness, dictators put the unemployed to work. The common man's standard of living in these states did not necessarily improve with employment, the more so because guns soon took precedence over butter when the communist and fascist states sought political objectives that were attainable only by force.

Dictators made a special appeal to youth. Young people were made to feel important, even indispensable to the nation's new ambitions. They were given special roles and special privileges as each nation tailored a new educational scheme, both in school and out, to promote the national interest. These nations pursued clearcut goals, although the goals were established by a central authority beyond the reach of the people.

The authoritarian states' singleminded pursuit of their national goals was in marked contrast with the wallowing of the democratic states. The authoritarian states had geared their educational efforts, in school and out, to their national goals with deadly efficiency at a time when the educational systems of the democracies were barely operational. Young people suffered, economically and emotionally, in a depressed society; they experienced by far the highest percentage of unemployment; they were not encouraged to attend school or college. It was the treatment of these phenomena which brought Dr. Peddiwell's lectures to a close.

This nation had lost its drive and momentum. President Coolidge proclaimed that "the business of America is business," but suddenly this simple explanation of the American ethos was challenged. The depression had economic manifestations which were almost overwhelming, but the attendant depression of the spirit was an even greater threat. There was little self-confidence, little self-respect, particularly among those who found it necessary to go on the dole. The economy had improved appreciably by 1939, when World War II started in Europe, but the United States Census of 1940 still counted 7.9 million unemployed. After Pearl Harbor, we simply set aside our domestic problems to get on with the war.

The Educational Scene

Although the founding fathers had made complimentary statements about education, there is serious doubt whether they comprehended the educational needs of a democratic society. The educational historian Good[1] has observed that Washington spoke of the need for enlightened public opinion; that Jefferson championed education as the preserver of liberty and civil rights; that the early

3

champion of public education, Horace Mann, promoted education for morality and economic efficiency. These were limited educational objectives at best: they did little to promote a comprehensive educational system or to develop school programs significantly different from those which prevailed in the monarchies of the Old World.

Education had been left to the states, but few states developed systems of education during the first fifty years of the nation's history. There were early gestures in the direction of educational support at the federal level, such as the Northwest Ordinance of 1787, which proclaimed the desirability of common schools and set aside land for their support. But opportunities for the masses to attend school were long delayed by the low density of the population outside the small cities of the Eastern Seaboard, by the unremitting hard work demanded of all in a frontier society, and by the learning opportunities apprenticeship offered in the economy of the day. A formal move for public education began to materialize in the 1840s, principally in the Northeast and in some settlements beyond the Alleghenies where the thrust of the Northeast was felt. Formal education also gained footholds in areas settled by those ethnic groups that had brought with them some of the more advanced educational practices of Europe.

Elementary schools remained ungraded outside the cities until 1860 — and five-sixths of the population then lived outside the cities. Textbooks were few and poorly written. Teacher preparation was almost completely neglected until after the Civil War, and it was marginally pursued until well into the Twentieth Century. While state after state proclaimed the principle of universal education, the principle remained unfulfilled for most children.

Public secondary education was delayed by the success of private academies, which served the needs of the affluent. It was not until 1880, and even later in most places, that public high schools were established. The public high school grew very rapidly between 1890 and 1930, doubling its population each decade. However, the accessibility of public education, both elementary and secondary, varied appreciably from state to state and from community to community within most states.

Education was dominated structurally by local administrative units and by local boards of control. As late as 1938, when *The Saber-Tooth Curriculum* was written, there were 118,892 organized local administrative units administering the public schools, serving approximately 221,660 public elementary schools and 25,467 public high schools. There were 11,957 units in Illinois

alone and 8,652 in Kansas.[2] More than half of all the school build-
ings in use in 1938 had only one room. High schools were small,
and their restricted size resulted in a restricted program. In 1938,
39 percent of all high schools had 99 pupils or fewer, and 76 percent had 299 pupils or fewer.[3] Some states kept fairly tight rein on
certain school matters such as records of attendance, textbook
selection, teacher certification, and recommended courses of study.
But with financing left principally to the local community, schools
remained what the local communities were willing to support.

By 1938 the theoretical base for education was reasonably sophis-
ticated, but the translation of theory into widespread practice was
impossible at the time. Our professional educators were well
acquainted with what had been said, written, and practiced elsewhere, and here and there there were educational breakthroughs.
Persons associated with education were among the first to perceive
that a democracy both implies and needs special educational opportunities.

Many instances could be cited in support of this observation. One
example is the National Herbart Society, which issued its first
publications in 1895. This society, inspired by the writings of the
German philosopher Johann Herbart (1776–1841), sought to make
education more scientific. Its members challenged the prevailing
faculty psychology and questioned the dictum that certain academic subjects are peculiarly suited to "training the mind." In 1902, as
the National Society for the Scientific Study of Education, and still
later as the National Society for the Study of Education (NSSE), it
became the nucleus of the "scientific movement" in education. The
NSSE issued yearbooks on courses of study, on the relation of
theory to practice in education and in teacher education, on teacher
certification, on the measurement of educational products, on intelligence tests and their use, on the education of gifted children—all before 1925. Some of this is suggestive of Peddiwell's
description of making education scientific "by counting and
measuring everything related to education which can be counted
and measured."

Vocational education at the secondary school level had received
a potential boost during World War I by way of federal legislation
known as the Smith-Hughes Vocational Education Act. The legislation was the first major sortie by the federal government into secondary education up until that time. However, there were few high
schools outside the cities large enough to support nonagricultural
programs, and the vocational-agriculture efforts in the rural areas
pursued an unrealistic "down-on-the-farm" concept which was

being denied by the economic realities. At the best the vocational offerings were unimaginative and school-centered in nature, and they were not regarded as having an important relationship to manpower training. We were a nation with a tradition of importing skilled labor, and we had accepted apprenticeship as our main vocational-training procedure, leaving secondary schools with only a small stake in the job-training arena.

Progressive education became a formal movement after World War I and reached the peak of its impact on elementary education in the late 1930s. Like earlier progressive movements in education, it gave more attention to the interest of the learner in the learning process, tried to relate instructional content to the needs of the learner, and attempted to use education as a means of individual development. To this John Dewey added the goal of making a better society. As early as 1899 Dewey had said to the parents of children in his laboratory school, "What the best and wisest parent wants for his own child, that must the community want for all of its children. Any other ideal for our schools is narrow and unlovely; acted upon, it destroys our democracy."[4]

As we entered the 1930s, our school effort was not a national thrust but a heterogeneity of systems with few common ties. There were national associations of teachers, administrators, and college professors; there were professional journals and yearbooks; there was some uniformity in teacher education although standards varied greatly. There were recommended courses of study developed principally by subject specialists; there was regional accreditation of secondary education and higher education. The educational approach within schools remained almost exclusively verbal-literary in content and method and book-centered in approach. Writers of the day stressed the need to recognize individual differences in aptitudes and capacities, and noted that these differences became greater as a higher percentage of students remained in school; they cited the impact of social changes on schools; they discussed the special role of the school in a democratic society. The sophistication of the literature was vastly superior to the practice; the promise was much greater than the reality.

When the economic underpinnings of the nation gave way, the institution through which a society re-creates itself was confused by the unclear goals and the unstated priorities of that society. It was in this educational setting that J. Abner Peddiwell, fortified by tequila daisies, delivered his famous lectures to a single student, Raymond Wayne.

The National Response

The political responses to the breakdown of the 1930s were, for the most part, specific responses to specific problems. They were intended to ameliorate a catastrophic situation and prevent the recurrence of conditions regarded as the root causes of the problems. The Reconstruction Finance Corporation, instituted during the Hoover administration, was a government lending agency designed to assist businesses in distress. During the early Roosevelt administration there were the Security and Exchange Commission to oversee the stock and bond markets (both having crashed), the National Industrial Recovery Act to stimulate business, the Agricultural Adjustment Administration to help the farmer, the National Labor Relations Board to aid the worker, the Federal Deposit Insurance Corporation to protect bank depositors. The Civil Works Administration provided money to local governmental units to put persons on payrolls; the Public Works Administration sponsored construction projects; and later the Works Progress Administration addressed itself to unemployment in all sectors. Social Security legislation was enacted to help the unemployed, the aged, and families without a breadwinner. The Home Owners Loan Corporation provided a loan resource for persons about to lose their homes, and the Federal Housing Act was loan insurance meant to encourage the construction of private homes.

So great were the pressures on the domestic front that there was little response to international developments. Japan entered the mainland of China unchallenged, Mussolini tried to conquer Ethiopia, and Hitler moved at will in central Europe. The United States paused in 1934 to recognize Russia, and Congress passed the Neutrality Act in 1935. Congress reaffirmed the act in subsequent years, forbidding loans to warring nations and requiring cash for goods sold to belligerents. There were other conditions, too, but the principle was a reaction against the World War I involvement and the bitter experience associated with war debts. For the time, domestic issues were almost overwhelming.

Earlier in the twentieth century there had, of course, been efforts to correct some of the abuses of the times and to provide the common man with a better break in life. Certain states had instituted reforms in the areas of child labor laws, workmen's compensation, length of work day and work week, health and safety conditions on the job, and old-age pensions. And, of course, school laws were the province of the individual state. States varied very widely in their legislative activity in these areas, but during the early part of the century the initiative for reform was exercised by the "progressive" states. Nationwide there was ballot reform which permitted secret voting, the election of United States senators by popular vote rather than by state legislatures, the Federal Reserve System, a modest but progressive income tax, and the extension of voting rights to women. Labor unions were developing stronger political and economic muscle once they dropped the baggage of social reformers and concentrated on improvements in wages, hours, and working conditions. They operated in an extralegal fashion since no federal law provided unions with access to formal negotiations procedures until passage of the National Labor Relations Act in 1935.

There was the urge to get to the heart of the problem, at least on the intellectual level. What were the major social developments? Could they be identified? President Hoover initiated a commission "to survey social changes in this country in order to throw light on the emerging problems which now confront us or which may be expected later to confront the people of the United States."

The introduction to The Hoover Commission's *Recent Social Trends,* published in 1933, cited problems that still face us in the 1970s. It reads in part as follows:

> Even a casual glance at some of these points of tension in our national life reveals a wide range of puzzling questions. Imperialism, peace or war, international relations, urbanism, trusts and mergers, crime and its prevention, taxation, social insurance, the plight of agriculture, foreign and domestic markets, governmental regulation of industry, shifting moral standards, new leadership in business and government, the status of womankind, labor, child training, mental hygiene, the future of democracy and capitalism, the reorganization of our governmental units, the use of leisure time, public and private medicine, better homes and standards of living—all of these and many others, for these are only samples taken from a long series of grave questions, demand attention if we are not to drift into zones of danger.[5]

The Hoover Commission had documented the ongoing social phenomena to which Harold Benjamin was reacting a few years later in *The Saber-Tooth Curriculum.*

During the 1930s there was a shift in the focus of government from the local and state level to the national level to cope with problems which the states and communities could not handle. States could not supervise the bond and stock markets; they could not underwrite bank deposits; they could not meet the welfare needs; they could not regulate interstate businesses when some single corporations controlled resources greater than those available to individual states; they could not manage industry-wide unions. A wave of investigations and studies was triggered in the hope that analysis might suggest remedies or solutions. Notable among them were the Hoover Commission's *Recent Social Trends*, previously mentioned; the Lynds' studies of class structure in a Midwestern community;[6] and Mumford's definitive work on the history, problems, and prospects of machine civilization.[7] The culminating economic study of the era was an investigation, by the Temporary National Economic Committee of the United States Senate, of the concentration of economic power in the United States.[8] This committee held hearings for two years and produced forty monographs. (Benjamin's Chapter V, "Education and Paleolithic Security," covers much the same ground.)

The nation had been forced to meet head-on the accumulated problems of an expanding industrial state which was endeavoring to operate within a democratic framework and a free-enterprise economy. The individual in the factory, in the mine, or on the farm was unable to cope with all the problems which confronted him. Eventually the nation as a whole could not bear what individuals had had to endure.

World War II, and our entry into the war in late 1941, interrupted the sequence of domestic developments which were underway, and the intensity of the experience and the gravity of the situation resulted in an unprecedented introspective examination. Studies and investigations revealed a rampant exploitation of the economy with little concern for the common welfare, a widespread misuse of natural resources, a serious breach between democratic principles and practices, a general absence of national goals, and an uncertainty about our proper role in international affairs. In education, progress had been made—the availability of elementary and secondary schooling had increased, and the land-grant college innovation was an unparalleled move to provide higher education to students of limited means. However, the educational system as a whole was almost completely inadequate for a technologically complex democratic society confronted by aggressive nations with radically different political and economic philosophies.

The Educational Response

In the 1930s the resources committed to education were woefully inadequate when measured against the nation's educational needs.

To repeat, the commonality in education resided in the activities of professional organizations, in the accepted design of a single ladder system of education, in the professional journals and other publications, and in on-the-job training opportunities inherent in many occupations. The state and local governments, which financed and administered the more than 118,000 school districts, were overwhelmed by the problems of financing relief and maintaining a few essential public services. Limited school budgets became even more restricted. Teachers felt the crunch either by way of salary reductions or salary moratoriums, along with spartan conditions in the classroom.

However, the fundamental frustration expressed satirically by Harold Benjamin in *The Saber-Tooth Curriculum* was caused by the wide gap between the prevailing practice and what was feasible; between the best and poorest practices; between the verbal commitment to education and the actual support it received; between the urgent need and the response.

By 1930 the broad outlines of the school-society relationship were fairly clear: many educators comprehended the special dependence of a democracy on its system of education. No one had expressed the features of the educational enterprise appropriate to a democracy better than John Dewey in his 1916 treatise, *Democracy and Education*. The opening sentence of Dewey's preface reads: "The following pages embody an endeavor to detect and to state the ideas implied in a democratic society and to apply these ideas to the problems of the enterprise of education."[9] Those who read this challenging book obtained a new vision of the role and possibilities of education, and this new vision attained its greatest popularity among the educators of the 1930s.

Educational literature of this period, as much as or more than other literature, championed the democratic way of life, although by this time an allegiance to democracy was in the mainstream of the American conscience. President Wilson's declaration of war, made on April 2, 1917, had included the statement "We shall fight for the things that we have always carried nearest our hearts — for democracy, for the right of those who submit to authority to have a voice in their own government."

School practices had improved in certain communities — usually affluent communities — with the result that superior practices could be observed and reported in useful ways. In these schools and communities it was recognized that the early childhood years constitute an extremely important period in the person's growth and development; attention was given to the emotional climate of the school;

2

special attention was given to exceptional children; curriculums
were more comprehensive; the physical plant was more nearly adequate; teachers were better qualified professionally and better in-
formed generally. Some of the keenest minds of the day were at-
tracted to education and particularly to the more profound aspects
of education—educational purposes, learning theory, and behavior
change. And even though the educational structure of the nation
was splintered into thousands of school districts, there was a fair
degree of professional cohesion made possible by well-organized
and well-administered groups and institutions.

The general theme of broad social purpose and relevance was ex-
pounded in preparatory materials for teachers and school administrators, and at a time when certification requirements brought
teachers and administrators to college and university campuses. In
1924, Chapman and Counts, captured the spirit thus:

> Greeting his pupils, the master asked:
>   What would you learn of me?
> And the reply came:
>   How shall we care for our bodies?
>   How shall we rear our children?
>   How shall we work together?
>   How shall we live with our fellowmen?
>   How shall we play?
>   For what ends shall we live?
> And the teacher pondered these words, and sorrow was in his heart, for
> his own learning touched not these things.[10]

The plight of the nation sharpened differences among the
Progressives. Progressive education had started as an educational
theory but spread as a practice, principally as the "activity movement" in the United States. This movement, confined largely to the
preschool and elementary school levels, featured teacher-pupil
planning, a variety of activities through which or around which content was presented, and an informal classroom arrangement and at-
mosphere. The "activity" schools usually developed instruction
around units such as community life, the home, and, almost invaria-
bly, Indians. The learner was the focus of attention in progressive
elementary schools, and learning experiences began with the child
at his stage of awareness and development. Secondary education
was much less responsive to the movement, but it did get as far as
experimenting with thirty schools in the "Eight-Year Study" which
began in 1933. The study, conducted by an arm of the Progressive
Education Association, popularized a few variations from current

practice, but the study by design was restricted to college-bound students.[11]

It was over the alleged emphasis on methodology and the neglect of broad social purpose that Progressives quarreled with fellow Progressives. Counts brought the issue into full view with a series of lectures which he titled: *Dare the Schools Build a New Social Order?* and by making such statements as: "To refuse to face the task of creating a vision of a future America immeasurably more just and noble and beautiful than the America of today is to evade the most crucial, difficult, and important educational task."[12] The early chapters of *The Saber-Tooth Curriculum* transpose the debate to the Stone Age, but the implication is clear that it applies to the present.

The Progressive movement had nearly run its course as an identifiable force in education by the time J. Abner Peddiwell was delivering his saber-tooth lectures. The same criticisms which Peddiwell cited were being leveled by outspoken critics within the movement. A general lack of basic philosophy could not be compensated for by circular statements such as "They learn to do by doing." Peddiwell made them sound even more ludicrous when he speaks of "learning what they live and living what they learn."

School people of the 1930s were fully aware of the special ways in which the depression affected children and youth. Teachers saw hungry and poorly clothed children day after day; they knew personally those students who dropped out of school for financial reasons or for the lack of attainable goals; teachers knew that youth had the highest unemployment rate. But school people were without ways and means of resolving either the immediate or longer-term problems of their students or of society.

Additional government agencies were created to meet the highly volatile youth problems which could not be disregarded without peril. The federal government entered the arena of education by way of these agencies. Between 1933 and 1936 approximately 40 percent of the employable youth between the ages of 16 and 24 were unemployed.[13]

First to the rescue was the Civilian Conservation Corps (CCC). The CCC was initiated in March 1933 and was administered by the Department of War. Its camps accepted men from 17 to $23^1/_2$ years old for periods of six months to two years. Eligibility rules required the candidate to be unmarried, out of work, and out of school. He received a cash allowance of $30 per month, half of which was sent home to his family. The nation was dotted with camps; in the peak year of 1935 there were 2,635 camps. The program was terminated in June 1942; during that interval the CCC served 3 million young men.

The men in the CCC camps were given on-the-job training in a variety of occupations. There was "book learning" too in the CCC camp, but it came in for criticism. A report by the Department of the Interior stated: ". . . .the Corps drifted gradually from job training to a school type of education for which neither the camp nor a large proportion of the enrollees was equipped."[14]

Next to appear was the National Youth Administration (NYA). The NYA was established by executive order in June 1935 as a nationwide undertaking. It was intended to serve youth of ages 16 to 25 as work training or by providing financial assistance earned through work while attending school or college. The wage payment averaged less than $20 per month. When terminated in December 1943, the NYA had employed 4,800,000 young people, 2,700,000 in work experience and 2,100,000 in school, college, or graduate school.[15]

Meanwhile, school people had begun to fear the threat of a parallel system of education dominated by the federal government. And many claimed that with the same resources the schools themselves could have mounted a better training program. The CCC and the NYA were subject to criticism because the work performed fell outside the enclosures of the marketplace and hence had busywork and "pork barrel" overtones.

Both the CCC and the NYA terminated just as the war effort was getting into full swing. Youth who had been a "problem" and who had needed job training were no longer a problem, but were desperately needed by the nation to wage war. The reports speak openly of how well the NYA training programs and how nicely the CCC camp experiences dovetailed with military activity. But the reports fall short of properly evaluating the agencies' performance in overcoming the underlying problems of job scarcity and the absence of universal opportunity for training and education.

Just as President Hoover sought to analyze the major social developments, the distinguished Educational Policies Commission of the National Education Association gave attention to the major educational issues of the day. The Association called upon Charles A. Beard to address the question of the role of education in a democracy, which he did in *The Unique Function of Education in American Democracy.* This work was completed in December 1936 and was published only months ahead of *The Saber-Tooth Curriculum.*

In his opening chapter Beard asked: "With the challenge of affairs, public and private, so urgent, what are the bearings by which to discover our position and chart our course? To what principles must we refer in discovering the task of education in American democracy?"[16] Beard enumerated five principles in answer to his own questions. Two of the five came very close to saying in "professional" style what Harold Benjamin covered in his description of the persistence of "fish-grabbing by the bare hand method," even when the streams were muddied by silt and gravel. These two principles of Beard's are:

2. Every system of thought and practice in education is formulated with some reference to the ideas and interests dominant or widely cherished in society at the time of its formulation.
3. Once created and systematized, any program of educational thought and practice takes on professional and institutional sterotypes, and tends to outlast even profound changes in the society in which it assumed its original shape.[17]

The Saber-Tooth Curriculum and *The Unique Function of Education in American Democracy* can be read side by side for their parallel perspective. The scope and point of view are much the same, ranging from the exaltation of education to the special oaths required of teachers as the nadir of educational esteem; from national self-confidence to a concern for the survival of the basic principles of individual freedom and responsibility.

Shortly after *The Saber-Tooth Curriculum* was published, World War II began. Soon our industries made us the "arsenal of democracy," and at the same time, 16 million men were inducted into service. We produced equipment and supplies sufficient to win the war with some margin to spare. One measure of the nation's technical competence was the rapid construction of an aircraft industry capable of producing 96,000 planes per year, even though the President's initial target of 50,000 planes seemed unrealistically high. We also trained crews to fly and maintain this vast air armada and to operate other equally complex war machines. These accomplishments were a direct tribute to the nation's educational capability; the payoff was much greater than anyone had a right to expect.

In one of his first postwar books Harold Benjamin contrasted our war efforts with our educational efforts: "When war comes. . .[man] serves it with all his might. He puts his life, his fortune, and his sacred honor into the balance. In our gaming idiom, he shoots the works."[18] Characterizing man's educational effort, Benjamin said: ". . . .he proceeds cautiously to confine education to a little book learning in the schools, doles it out in bargain lots to groups privileged in various economic and social ways, and leaves the bulk of its work to be done by agencies and individuals with special behavior-changing goals of their own. He serves education timidly, giving it occasional handouts and pledging it a carefully limited literacy. He does not shoot the works. He shoots two bits and then complains that his winnings are small."[19]

Since Harold Benjamin wrote those words, *structural* process, at any rate, has been made. Schools have been consolidated; most of them are now sufficiently large to permit comprehensive programs. Only 4,000 one-room elementary schools remained in 1968, compared with 107,000 in 1940. States have assumed the leadership in education (although a little more than half of the school financing continues to come from local political units). Total expenditures for all formal education amounted to $65 billion in 1970, compared with $3.2 billion in 1940. Forty-five percent of the 18–21 age group is enrolled in college. However, misalignment between what can be done in and through education and what is accomplished continues to plague the nation. Perhaps at the peak of our effort to date we also have our most serious reservations and concerns about the effectiveness of education.

There is at least one ray of hope. Recent reports on alcoholic consumption reveal a sharp increase in the use of tequila. If a few "tequila daisies" working on the mind of J. Abner Peddiwell produced *The Saber-Tooth Curriculum*, there is always the chance that this great personality expander, properly used in a favorable setting, will permit someone else to write a sequel.

R. Lee Hornbake
Vice President for Academic Affairs
University of Maryland

Notes

1. H. G. Good, *A History of American Education*, 2d ed., p.353. New York: The Macmillan Company, 1962.

2. U.S. Office of Education, Biennial Survey of Education in the United States. *Statistics of State School Systems, 1937–38,* Bulletin 1940, no. 2, chap. II, pp. 2–3.

3. U.S. Office of Education, Biennial Survey of Education in the United States. *Statistics of Public High Schools, 1937–38*, Bulletin 1940, no. 2, chap. V., p. 5.

4. John Dewey, *The School and Society.* Chicago: The University of Chicago Press. (The first three chapters were lectures delivered in April 1899; the initial publication date was November 1899.)

5. President's (Hoover) Committee on Recent Social Trends, *Recent Social Trends in the United States*, pp. xi-xii. New York: McGraw-Hill Book Company, 1933.

6. Robert S. Lynd and Helen M. Lynd, *Middletown: A Study in Contemporary American Culture.* New York: Harcourt, Brace and Company, Inc., 1929; *Middletown in Transition: A Study in Cultural Conflicts.* New York: Harcourt, Brace & World, Inc., 1937.

7. Lewis Mumford, *Technics and Civilization.* New York: Harcourt, Brace and Company, Inc., 1934.

8. United States Senate (Temporary National Economic Committee), *Investigation of Concentration of Economic Power.* Washington, D.C., 1941. (This reference is to 40 monographs. For convenience see *Final Report and Recommendations of the Temporary National Economic Committee*).

9. John Dewey, *Democracy and Education.* New York: The Macmillan Company, 1916.

10. J. Crosby Chapman and George S. Counts, *Principles of Education.* Boston: Houghton Mifflin Company, 1924.

11. Wilford M. Aiken, *The Story of the Eight-Year Study*, New York: Harper & Brothers, 1942.

12. Counts, *Dare the School Build a New Social Order?* New York: John Day Co., 1932, p. 55.

13. Homer P. Rainey, et al., *How Fare American Youth?* p. 34. New York: D. Appleton-Century Company, Inc., 1937.

14. U.S. Department of the Interior, *Civilian Conservation Program of the Department of the Interior, March 1933 to June 30, 1943*, p. 3. Washington, D.C., 1945.

15. U.S. Federal Security Agency, *Final Report of the National Youth Administration (Fiscal Years 1936–1943)*, p. 1. Washington, D.C., 1944.

16. National Education Association, Educational Policies Commission, *The Unique Function of Education in American Democracy*, p. 6. Washington, D.C., 1937.

17. Ibid.

18. Harold Benjamin, *Under Their Own Command*, p. 1. New York: The Macmillan Company, 1947.

19. Ibid., p. 2.

SABER-TOOTH

. . . . Including Other Lectures in the

by J. ABNER PEDDIWELL, PH.D.
and SEVERAL TEQUILA DAISIES

McGRAW-HILL BOOK COMPANY, INC.

CURRICULUM

History of Paleolithic Education . . . .

as told to RAYMOND WAYNE
with a Foreword by HAROLD BENJAMIN
NEW YORK AND LONDON

13 14 - MU - 9

49151

DEDICATION

*To the Two Young Professors Who Shared My Office
in the Summer of the Paper Famine*

DEAR COLLEAGUES:

Ordinarily a dedication is merely a gesture of affection.
In the present case, it is that and also an accusation of
being accessories before the fact, for I must charge you
with grave responsibility for the manner and substance
of these lectures. They were cast in narrative form to hold
your fickle attention; they avoid a definite tendency toward the educational left in deference to your youthful
conservatism; and they are brief because you borrowed
most of my paper.

Yours sincerely,

THE AUTHOR

FOREWORD

I HAVE read the following narrative and find it faintly amusing in spots. Perhaps there are even some theoretical suggestions of not wholly negligible significance beneath the fantastic and outlandish exterior.

I must raise several grave questions, however, concerning the professional standing, general reliability, and, to speak quite bluntly, the veracity of the author or authors. I have consulted various biographical directories and the membership lists of some of the most important educational organizations, and I fail to find any evidence whatever of the existence of a man named J. Abner Peddiwell. If there is a man of that name, I doubt that he is a professor of education. Furthermore, I have examined the most recent edition of the national directory of institutions of higher education, published by the United States Office of Education, and I am unable to discover any mention of the Petaluma State College of whose faculty the so-called Professor Peddiwell is allegedly a member.

It seems probable, therefore, that these *soisant-dit* lectures are solely the work of the flashily dressed young man who submitted the manuscript to me in person. My secretary granted him an interview with me under the impression that he was, at best, a sales representative of one of the college textbook publishing companies or, at worst, a life insurance salesman. He entered my office breezily, greeted me familiarly, said his name was Raymond Wayne, and claimed to have been one of my students some ten years ago.

When I asked this self-assured young man to leave an address to which I might forward my comments on the manuscript, he refused to do so on the following grounds: (1) the nature of his business was such that he had no permanent address, (2) he knew without any comments from me that the manuscript was good, and (3) he

viii

could learn of the publication of the book by reading laudatory reviews of it in professional journals.

Although the man's extreme assurance irritated me beyond ordinary measure, I controlled my resentment and asked him how it would be possible to send him his royalties in the event of the manuscript's publication and in the further event that anyone should buy the book after publication. He replied that he desired me to collect the royalties and use them for giving professors of education some basic training in methods of teaching.

"Do you expect the hypothetical royalties from this hypothetical publication to be large enough for such a noble purpose?" I asked sarcastically.

"Frankly, no," he replied. "It would take all the resources of the Carnegie Foundation for the Advancement of Teaching even to make a beginning on a job as big as that. But it's the principle of the thing I want to establish. You spend the first fifty thousand of my royalties on the project, and then maybe each of the big foundations will kick in a million or two apiece and we'll get somewhere."

ix

This is probably an adequate sampling of the man's attitude toward the whole system of modern education. The more important question of his reliability may easily be checked against some of his specific statements.

The author claims in his introductory chapter that he is a member of Phi Beta Kappa and received the baccalaureate degree with great distinction. Although I cannot refute this statement by appeal to documents, I must insist that indirect evidence from the manuscript itself leads to the inescapable conclusion that the person who wrote it possessed neither the coveted key nor the arts degree *magna cum laude*. The contempt displayed by the author for many of the basic principles underlying the academic processes leading to these distinctions is in itself sufficient to stamp him as one whose own education, on the liberal side at least, was sadly neglected. In fact it is difficult to resist the suspicion that the man who wrote the following pages does not believe that the great cultural verities are eternal, changeless, possessing a certain indefinable and imponderable something whose essence is timelessness.

In conclusion, therefore, I submit this work with the following summary of my judgments concerning the authorship claimed on the title page.

There is no professor of education named J. Abner Peddiwell.

The man who calls himself Raymond Wayne is probably antagonistic to liberal culture and is almost certainly a liar.

The "Several Tequila Daisies" mentioned as coauthors of this narrative apparently involve the alcoholic phase of the presentation, comment on which is beneath my contempt.

HAROLD BENJAMIN.

xi

CONTENTS

Foreword by Harold Benjamin   *vii*

I   Seminar in Tijuana   *3*

II   The Saber-Tooth Curriculum   *24*

III   The Real-Tiger School   *45*

IV   Higher Paleolithic Education   *74*

V   Education and Paleolithic Security   *93*

VI   The Paleolithic Youth Problem   *111*

VII   The Disintegration of Dr. Peddiwell   *128*

xiii

THE SABER-TOOTH CURRICULUM

1 · SEMINAR IN TIJUANA

THE longest bar in the world, as I suppose almost everybody knows, is in Tijuana. It is on the left side of the main street just after you cross the border looking for relaxation. If you stand at the middle of that bar and look to right and left long enough with a pair of field glasses, you will eventually see everyone in the world who believes that tequila daisies and relaxation go together. Of course, you would never expect to find there a man who was ignorant of both terms in that famous pair of remedies for mental and spiritual malaise, yet that is what happened to me when I had my last near approach to a nervous breakdown and was easily persuaded

3

to take a two weeks' vacation south of the border.

It was my first day in Tijuana. I had just ordered one more tequila daisy and was gazing at the starboard wing of the bar with what seemed to be a clear and untroubled vision when I saw a sober brown suit on a compact but rotund figure approach the bar about fifty meters from where I was stationed. A decade earlier, during my upper division work at the Petaluma State College, that suit and the personality which gave it meaning and character had been hammered into my consciousness five hours a week, forty weeks a year, until my response to them was automatic.

At first I stared in disbelief. My reason told me that this phenomenon could not be in Tijuana; that, most of all, it was impossible in a place selling liquor. Despite the evidence of my eyes and memory, it seemed certain that what I was experiencing was merely an illusion occasioned by the impact of tequila daisies on deeply carved neural pathways.

"Luis," I called, "how many daisies have I had?"

4

"Eet ees onlee your fort' wan," the bartender answered, a little reproachfully, as though it was hardly yet time for me to become talkative.

I looked again, and there the illusion still stood, leaning against the bar, waiting for service.

"Do you see a short, fattish bird in a funny looking brown suit up the bar there a ways?" I asked.

Luis looked and nodded. "Beer," he diagnosed sadly, "joos' to say he ees dreenk at de longes' bar een de worl'."

"Beer!" I repeated. "Never! Not a drop of alcohol in any form if that man is who I think he is. Beat it up there, Luis, and get his order. Quick!"

Luis obeyed slowly, mumbling as he went, "Alcohol, hell! Beer ees joos' beer."

The four tequila daisies could not have been enough to blur or otherwise distort my vision. It must have been an excess of emotion that caused me momentarily to lose sight of Luis and the customer in the brown suit. I waited, supporting my body against the bar, my heart pounding in my throat. If by some miracle the impossible had

5

happened and the hero of my university days was really in this place, I knew that I should have to pay my respects, even though running the risk of having tequila smelled on my breath.

At length Luis's face, steered by its long mustaches, loomed again through the fog across the bar.

"What did he order?" I demanded hoarsely.

"Notheeng," replied Luis disgustedly. "He joos' weesh to know how een hell we are sure dees ees longes' bar een de worl'. W'ere een hell ees our proof, he say."

"Did he—did he actually say *hell?*" I asked almost in a whisper.

"Oh, no. *I* am say *hell.* De professor, he speak deeferent, but w'at he wan' to know ees how een hell we—"

"*Professor?* Did he say he was a professor?"

"Sure—he claim he ees professor een Petaluma Colegio, an' he wan' to know how een hell—"

Luis's voice faded into a receding monotone while I straightened my necktie, pulled down my vest, and set my hat in square respectability. The miracle had happened. I would have paid my

6

"*If you ask me to prove that it is the longest bar in the world, I shall ask you to prove that it is not the longest.*"

7

respects, if necessary, through a barrier of forty tequila daisies. The pleasant, warm mist of a trifling four could not deter me for a moment.

"Dr. Peddiwell," I began as I approached the great scholar, who was still waiting for evidence to support the bar's claim of dimensional superiority.

He turned and touched his hat with characteristic courtesy. "Your face is familiar," he said automatically, "but I am afraid I—"

"Wayne—Raymond Wayne," I supplied, removing my hat. "You won't remember me, Doctor, but I was in your classes at Petaluma ten years ago, and I—"

"Of course, *of course!*" He shook my hand warmly. "Your name, sir, was right on the tip of my tongue. Remember you? Why certainly I remember you. An *A* student, you were, if my memory does not play me false."

"Yes, sir, and Phi Beta Kappa," I murmured modestly.

"Of course, of *course.*"

"A. B., *magna cum laude*," I continued.

"Certainly, of *course.*"

8

"Major in history of education."

"Well, well! My own field! Of course I remember you, Mr.—Mr.—"

"Wayne—Raymond Wayne."

"Mr. Wayne, of *course*. And where are you teaching now?"

"Well, Doctor, I—er—I am not—er—teaching anywhere at present."

"Not teaching? That's terrible! Major in History of Education—*A* student—everything. We must find a teaching position for you at once."

"Well—I haven't been looking for a teaching position for several years."

"You haven't? But—what are you—what is your—?"

"I—I am selling electric washing machines."

"A traveling salesman?"

"Well, in a certain way, yes."

"Of *course*, many advantages in that line of endeavor, I can see at once."

"A few, yes, sir—money, for instance."

"Er—quite so—and travel—you see a good many towns and cities in your journeys about the country, do you not?"

9

"Well, some, yes."

"And these—er—bars also?"

"Why—sometimes—yes. You know, Doctor—entertaining prospects, having sales conferences—that sort of thing."

"Ah, yes. And is it your judgment, on the basis of your observations, that this is actually the longest bar in the world?"

"It's the longest one *I* ever saw, Doctor."

"Excuse my insistence, but have you ever measured it?"

"Well—er—no."

"Have you ever measured any other bar?"

"Why, no, I don't believe I ever have."

"Ah, then—forgive any semblance of cross-examination—how do you *know* that this is the longest bar in the world?" He paused pityingly. Then, without waiting for an answer, wishing in his kindly way to spare me further embarrassment, he hastened on, "I shall not press the point to a tiresome length, but you grasp the issue, Mr.—Mr.—?"

"Wayne," I supplied automatically, grateful for being permitted once more to see that flawless intellect in operation.

"Of *course*, Mr. Wayne. You took my course in History of the Science of Education, did you not?"

"Yes, sir, I took *all* your courses."

"You will perhaps remember my lecture on the testing of hypotheses?"

"Doctor, I remember *all* your lectures."

"Thank you, sir. You recall the central proposition in that lecture?"

"Well—er—I . . . "

"Briefly stated, it ran to the general effect that education becomes scientific in proportion to the increasing willingness of educationists to test their hypotheses."

"Yes, sir."

"Very well. The hypothesis concerning the length of this bar offers an interesting example. Here we have hundreds of tourists daily, perhaps, all of whom are told and many of whom believe that this is the longest bar in the world. These tourists are being educated through the medium of an hypothesis, an untested hypothesis, an hypothesis unsupported by objective evidence, an hypothesis naked of precise data. In this regard, therefore, the curriculum for these tourists is medieval. It is a faith-conjecture-guess curriculum

11

built on a maximum of speculation and a minimum of exact observation. What is needed in the Tijuana-tourist educational system, as in other more formal systems all over the world, is an increase in careful measurement, and a decrease in fantastic humbug!"

Peddiwell liked critical ability in his students, so I was ready with an argument as soon as he paused.

"With your main proposition," I said, "there can be no quarrel. The testing of hypotheses is an ultimate necessity in any science. It seems possible, however, that you are minimizing the importance of the initial hypothesis. We need some fantastic conjectures at first in order later to have anything to test. We must first be subjective in a large way in order that we may afterward become objective in the grand manner. We should not forget that the wildest hypothesis may conceivably serve a useful scientific purpose more effectively than a hundred researchers working with objective scores from a thousand tests, aided by ten thousand statisticians with a hundred thousand calculating machines, grinding out a million correlations, ten

12

million probable errors, a hundred million indexes of the significance of differences, a billion—''

I hesitated, becoming suddenly aware that the professor was looking at me curiously and that the figures I was quoting, as well as the pitch of my voice, both of them a trifle stepped up by four daisies, were becoming somewhat extravagant.

"Take the hypothesis concerning the length of this bar," I continued in a more moderate tone. "Here we have a specific instance of an untested generalization with great potential utility. You neglect, for example, the potentially important social purpose served by this hypothesis."

"Indeed!" He raised his eyebrows. "May I ask what useful purpose could possibly be served by an hypothesis relating to grandiose claims to bigness of an agency devoted to the dispensing of alcoholic liquors?"

By this time I could see quite clearly that the tequila I had slapped rather hurriedly on a relatively empty stomach was beginning to accelerate my mental processes and lower the threshold of my inhibitions. My formally educated cerebrum noted this fact and counseled caution, but my

13

daisy-educated, subcortical self gave an inner whoop of delight and tossed caution overboard.

"The integration of the human personality, Doctor, that's the answer," I said.

The great man stared at me coldly. "It is a well-known fact, sir," he began, "that alcohol, even when consumed in minute quantities, has depressive if not actually deleterious effects on the—"

The daisies got behind me and pushed me into an interruption. "Physiologically," I announced, "only physiologically, and then only when we define the term in a narrow and non-organismic way. With a minor physiological effect, however, we are not concerned. We are students of behavior-modifying goals, agencies, instruments, procedures. We are educationists, which is to say applied psychologists. We work with men—men in action—men in action directed towards the betterment of their lives!"

The professor expelled air violently through the nose. "Humph! Those verbalizations may be all right for an introductory course, but here and now I want something specific."

14

"All right, Doctor, here's an instance. Consider the case of a downtrodden tourist—a traveling Joe Doakes from Podunkville—a man accustomed in his usual habitat to being small potatoes, browbeaten by a domineering boss and snapped into line by a strong-willed wife, a man who gets his political opinions from Mr. Hearst's hireling pundits and his economic views from Colonel McCormick, a man who is perforce satisfied to live in a small place, work at a small job, and occupy an inferior status in general."

"A sad picture," observed the professor sympathetically, "and one which in certain respects fits many a man whom the world regards as occupying an important position and holding superior status. I have known a Governor Joe Doakes, several Captain Doakeses, and in the academic world, sir, the name of Doakes might well be borne even by certain deans and presidents."

"Exactly, Doctor, but consider the case of this hypothetical little man a trifle further. Everything in his existence combines to make him feel unimportant. His personality becomes disintegrated. And *then*, Doctor, this individual is enabled to

point

15

come to Tijuana for a vacation. He is able to come alone, without his wife or other representative of authority. He comes into this barroom and—"

"Of course, of *course*," interrupted the professor briskly. "I see—no wife—no boss—freedom— personality expands and integrates—but—"

"He comes into this barroom," I continued hurriedly, "and at once the management does the socially valuable thing. It tells him he is in a unique place, not uniquely unimportant like himself, but uniquely great as he does not dare to dream of being. Under the impact of this suggestion his personality begins to unfold and blossom like a drought-withered flower under a cooling, gentle rain."

"Yes, yes," said the professor approvingly. "Quite neatly, even artistically, put, but you cannot gainsay the damning fact that this place is devoted to the sale of alcohol, and your pathetic little man will be tempted to—"

"Quite so, and that is a part of the treatment. The barroom suggests to our little, unimportant hero that he can become a part of this uniquely great phenomenon by drinking at the bar. There-

16

fore, he drinks—maybe beer, in which case his personality becomes a trifle better integrated; maybe wine, which helps his personality somewhat more; maybe hard liquor, like whiskey or rum, whereupon he may become markedly integrated; or maybe, if he is fortunate, tequila in the form known as the tequila daisy, which expands his personality in a uniquely effective manner."

"And—er—what is tequila?"

"It is a distilled liquor, a spirit—spirit is a good word—it is the liquid soul of certain varieties of the *maguey* plant. Among the derivatives of *maguey*, tequila stands supreme as an integrator of the human personality."

Up to that moment I had assumed that the discussion was purely academic. You will understand my astonishment, therefore, at the professor's next move. Deliberately he stepped away from the bar and regarded himself at one of the image-distorting mirrors along the back wall. Slowly he loosened his necktie. With a kind of precise carelessness he unbuttoned the coat of that famous brown suit. With obvious satisfaction he looked

17

at the abnormally elongated and slender figure which the trick mirror gave him. Gravely he turned to where I stood waiting.

"If you don't mind," he announced, "I will have one of these tequila daisies."

A fear clutched my throat, a fear that I might faint before I could give the order for the drink, a fear that I might thus miss seeing the first contact between two great spirits. But some measure of the courage of my fighting ancestors carried me through. I called Luis and ordered two tequila daisies.

"My wife," remarked Dr. Peddiwell at the end of his first daisy, "is in San Diego, Mr.—er—"

"Wayne," I said, recalling the image of a most determined-looking woman who had seemed to dislike me thoroughly whenever she had seen me in her husband's seminar.

"Of *course*. Yes, sir, my wife is attending a national convention of the League of American Needlewomen. She is an official delegate from the Petaluma chapter or local of that organization.

Indeed, if my memory does not play me false, she is chairman of the state committee on the relationship between economic planning and cross-stitching."

"Ah, very interesting," I commented politely, "and—er—exciting, too, for Mrs. Peddiwell, no doubt, and—ah—probably quite useful as well— needle craft and all that sort of thing." I labored heavily, wishing that the professor would not dwell on the activities of that woman. I did not care whether she was in San Diego or in a locality reputed to have a much less comfortable climate. With five daisies under my belt, moreover, I hated to pretend that I did care.

"And do you know where *I* am at the present time?" pursued the professor.

"In Tijuana, Baja California, Republica Mexicana," I replied promptly, the daisies giving me a good Castilian accent.

"In a certain objective and geographically tested sense, yes," agreed Peddiwell, "but in a more hypothetical and maritally correct sense, no. So far as Mrs. Peddiwell is concerned, I am at this

19

moment and for the rest of the week in the library of the University of California at Berkeley engaged in scholarly labors."

I looked at the man with a new respect. My old adolescent admiration for him was enriched and enhanced by a mature delight in the unsuspected depths of his character. A man who could lie so completely to that lantern-jawed Mrs. Peddiwell and get away with it was one whom I could follow to hell through a great forest of tequila daisies. I had an impulse to climb upon the bar and declaim his praises, but I inhibited this reaction as being undignified and was just about to indicate to the bartender that our glasses were empty when Dr. Peddiwell anticipated me.

"Luis," he called, slapping the bar with his open hand in a most emphatic manner, "two more daisies—and kindly snap out of your dope!"

At the end of the second round, the professor's usual fleeting and delicate smile had assumed a certain degree of careless permanency and robustness. He set down his glass and regarded me benignly. "I wish to say frankly," he stated in full lecture-room voice, "that I now appreciate your

20

point of view concerning the social value of certain fantastic and unsupported hypotheses. May I ask whether you have considerable time to spend in this place?"

"Two weeks, Doctor."

"Good, I have five days. The time is adequate though not excessive. The student body is well educated in the fundamentals—one hundred per cent Phi Beta Kappa. The lecture room is the longest of its kind in the world. If you ask me to prove that it is the longest, I shall ask you to prove that it is not the longest. The instructor is, I hope, not altogether unprepared. Under these circumstances, I propose a seminar—in the history of paleolithic education—hypothetical, fantastic, conjectural—lectures and discussion—no term reports or—Luis! *Que hombre!* Don't you see these empty glasses?"

At the end of the doctor's third daisy, which you must remember was the seventh one for me, I confess that my own frame of reference was becoming a bit unreal. I could catch only a sentence or two as they came dancing by in gay circles.

21

"Mr.—er—your confounded name seems to elude me," observed the professor, wiping a daisy drop off his lapel, "that is to say, your surname eludes me. What is your Christian name?"

"Chris'—Chris'n name?"

"Yes, your first name, you know."

"Oh! Firs' name? Firs' name's Ray—Raymon'."

"Raymond? Ah, hell! That is more difficult to remember than your last name! Hereafter, with your permission, I shall call you Bill—or Pete."

"'S'all ri' with me, old-timer," I assured him. "Don' give a double-edge' damn what you call me jus' so long's you lecture on hist'ry of pale—pal—lithya—*that* kind of education."

"I'll start tomorrow," he told me, "when my class is somewhat more on its intellectual toes, as it were."

I do not know whether we had any more daisies on that occasion. A careful search of my memory for the remainder of the evening yields only two fragments. One of them glimpses Dr. Peddiwell hailing a passing schoolma'am tourist from the United States as "Bright eyes"; the other reveals

22

him singing lullabies to me in a taxicab on our way to the hotel in Agua Caliente—at least the tunes were reminiscent of lullabies, although the words appeared to be derived in part from the professor's early experiences as a whistle-pup in an Oregon logging camp.

23

II · THE SABER-TOOTH CURRICULUM

THE first great educational theorist and practitioner of whom my imagination has any record (began Dr. Peddiwell in his best professorial tone) was a man of Chellean times whose full name was *New-Fist-Hammer-Maker* but whom, for convenience, I shall hereafter call *New-Fist*.

New-Fist was a doer, in spite of the fact that there was little in his environment with which to do anything very complex. You have undoubtedly heard of the pear-shaped, chipped-stone tool which archeologists call the *coup-de-poing* or fist hammer. New-Fist gained his name and a considerable local prestige by producing one of these artifacts in

24

a less rough and more useful form than any previously known to his tribe. His hunting clubs were generally superior weapons, moreover, and his fire-using techniques were patterns of simplicity and precision. He knew how to do things his community needed to have done, and he had the energy and will to go ahead and do them. By virtue of these characteristics he was an educated man.

New-Fist was also a thinker. Then, as now, there were few lengths to which men would not go to avoid the labor and pain of thought. More readily than his fellows, New-Fist pushed himself beyond those lengths to the point where cerebration was inevitable. The same quality of intelligence which led him into the socially approved activity of producing a superior artifact also led him to engage in the socially disapproved practice of thinking. When other men gorged themselves on the proceeds of a successful hunt and vegetated in dull stupor for many hours thereafter, New-Fist ate a little less heartily, slept a little less stupidly, and arose a little earlier than his comrades to sit by the fire and think. He would stare moodily at the flickering flames and wonder about various parts

25

of his environment until he finally got to the point where he became strongly dissatisfied with the accustomed ways of his tribe. He began to catch glimpses of ways in which life might be made better for himself, his family, and his group. By virtue of this development, he became a dangerous man.

This was the background that made this doer and thinker hit upon the concept of a conscious, systematic education. The immediate stimulus which put him directly into the practice of education came from watching his children at play. He saw these children at the cave entrance before the fire engaged in activity with bones and sticks and brightly colored pebbles. He noted that they seemed to have no purpose in their play beyond immediate pleasure in the activity itself. He compared their activity with that of the grown-up members of the tribe. The children played for fun; the adults worked for security and enrichment of their lives. The children dealt with bones, sticks, and pebbles; the adults dealt with food, shelter, and clothing. The children protected themselves

26

"They are living what they learn, and learning what they live."

27

57

from boredom; the adults protected themselves from danger.

"If I could only get these children to do the things that will give more and better food, shelter, clothing, and security," thought New-Fist, "I would be helping this tribe to have a better life. When the children became grown, they would have more meat to eat, more skins to keep them warm, better caves in which to sleep, and less danger from the striped death with the curving teeth that walks these trails by night."

Having set up an educational goal, New-Fist proceeded to construct a curriculum for reaching that goal. "What things must we tribesmen know how to do in order to live with full bellies, warm backs, and minds free from fear?" he asked himself.

To answer this question, he ran various activities over in his mind. "We have to catch fish with our bare hands in the pool far up the creek beyond that big bend," he said to himself. "We have to catch fish with our bare hands in the pool right at the bend. We have to catch them in the same way in the pool just this side of the bend. And so we catch them in the next pool and the next and

28

the next. Always we catch them with our bare hands."

Thus New-Fist discovered the first subject of the first curriculum—fish-grabbing-with-the-bare-hands.

parts of curric.

"Also we club the little woolly horses," he continued with his analysis. "We club them along the bank of the creek where they come down to drink. We club them in the thickets where they lie down to sleep. We club them in the upland meadow where they graze. Wherever we find them we club them."

So woolly-horse-clubbing was seen to be the second main subject in the curriculum.

"And finally, we drive away the saber-tooth tigers with fire," New-Fist went on in his thinking. "We drive them from the mouth of our caves with fire. We drive them from our trail with burning branches. We wave firebrands to drive them from our drinking hole. Always we have to drive them away, and always we drive them with fire."

Thus was discovered the third subject—saber-tooth-tiger-scaring-with-fire.

29

Having developed a curriculum, New-Fist took his children with him as he went about his activities. He gave them an opportunity to practice these three subjects. The children liked to learn. It was more fun for them to engage in these purposeful activities than to play with colored stones just for the fun of it. They learned the new activities well, and so the educational system was a success.

As New-Fist's children grew older, it was plain to see that they had an advantage in good and safe living over other children who had never been educated systematically. Some of the more intelligent members of the tribe began to do as New-Fist had done, and the teaching of fish-grabbing, horse-clubbing, and tiger-scaring came more and more to be accepted as the heart of real education.

For a long time, however, there were certain more conservative members of the tribe who resisted the new, formal educational system on religious grounds. "The Great Mystery who speaks in thunder and moves in lightning," they announced impressively, "the Great Mystery who gives men life and takes it from them as he wills—

30

if that Great Mystery had wanted children to practice fish-grabbing, horse-clubbing, and tiger-scaring before they were grown up, he would have taught them these activities himself by implanting in their natures instincts for fish-grabbing, horse-clubbing, and tiger-scaring. New-Fist is not only impious to attempt something the Great Mystery never intended to have done; he is also a damned fool for trying to change human nature."

Whereupon approximately half of these critics took up the solemn chant, "If you oppose the will of the Great Mystery, you must die," and the remainder sang derisively in unison, "You can't change human nature."

Being an educational statesman as well as an educational administrator and theorist, New-Fist replied politely to both arguments. To the more theologically minded, he said that, as a matter of fact, the Great Mystery had ordered this new work done, that he even did the work himself by causing children to want to learn, that children could not learn by themselves without divine aid, that they could not learn at all except through the power of the Great Mystery, and that nobody could really

31

understand the will of the Great Mystery concerning fish, horses, and saber-tooth tigers unless he
had been well grounded in the three fundamental
subjects of the New-Fist school. To the human-
nature-cannot-be-changed shouters, New-Fist
pointed out the fact that paleolithic culture had
attained its high level by changes in human
nature and that it seemed almost unpatriotic to
deny the very process which had made the community great.

"I know you, my fellow tribesmen," the pioneer
educator ended his argument gravely, "I know you
as humble and devoted servants of the Great
Mystery. I know that you would not for one
moment consciously oppose yourselves to his will.
I know you as intelligent and loyal citizens of this
great cave-realm, and I know that your pure and
noble patriotism will not permit you to do anything which will block the development of that
most cave-realmish of all our institutions—the
paleolithic educational system. Now that you
understand the true nature and purpose of this
institution, I am serenely confident that there are

32

no reasonable lengths to which you will not go in its defense and its support."

By this appeal the forces of conservatism were won over to the side of the new school, and in due time everybody who was anybody in the community knew that the heart of good education lay in the three subjects of fish-grabbing, horse-clubbing, and tiger-scaring. New-Fist and his contemporaries grew old and were gathered by the Great Mystery to the Land of the Sunset far down the creek. Other men followed their educational ways more and more, until at last all the children of the tribe were practiced systematically in the three fundamentals. Thus the tribe prospered and was happy in the possession of adequate meat, skins, and security.

It is to be supposed that all would have gone well forever with this good educational system if conditions of life in that community had remained forever the same. But conditions changed, and life which had once been so safe and happy in the cave-realm valley became insecure and disturbing.

A new ice age was approaching in that part of the world. A great glacier came down from the

33

neighboring mountain range to the north. Year after year it crept closer and closer to the head-waters of the creek which ran through the tribe's valley, until at length it reached the stream and began to melt into the water. Dirt and gravel which the glacier had collected on its long journey were dropped into the creek. The water grew muddy. What had once been a crystal-clear stream in which one could see easily to the bottom was now a milky stream into which one could not see at all.

At once the life of the community was changed in one very important respect. It was no longer possible to catch fish with the bare hands. The fish could not be seen in the muddy water. For some years, moreover, the fish in this creek had been getting more timid, agile, and intelligent. The stupid, clumsy, brave fish, of which originally there had been a great many, had been caught with the bare hands for fish generation after fish generation, until only fish of superior intelligence and agility were left. These smart fish, hiding in the muddy water under the newly deposited glacial boulders, eluded the hands of the most expertly

34

trained fish-grabbers. Those tribesmen who had studied advanced fish-grabbing in the secondary school could do no better than their less well-educated fellows who had taken only an elementary course in the subject, and even the university graduates with majors in ichthyology were baffled by the problem. No matter how good a man's fish-grabbing education had been, he could not grab fish when he could not find fish to grab.

The melting waters of the approaching ice sheet also made the country wetter. The ground became marshy far back from the banks of the creek. The stupid woolly horses, standing only five or six hands high and running on four-toed front feet and three-toed hind feet, although admirable objects for clubbing, had one dangerous characteristic. They were ambitious. They all wanted to learn to run on their middle toes. They all had visions of becoming powerful and aggressive animals instead of little and timid ones. They dreamed of a far-distant day when some of their descendants would be sixteen hands high, weigh more than half a ton, and be able to pitch their would-be riders into the dirt. They knew they

35

could never attain these goals in a wet, marshy country, so they all went east to the dry, open plains, far from the paleolithic hunting grounds. Their places were taken by little antelopes who came down with the ice sheet and were so shy and speedy and had so keen a scent for danger that no one could approach them closely enough to club them.

The best trained horse-clubbers of the tribe went out day after day and employed the most efficient techniques taught in the schools, but day after day they returned empty-handed. A horse-clubbing education of the highest type could get no results when there were no horses to club.

Finally, to complete the disruption of paleolithic life and education, the new dampness in the air gave the saber-tooth tigers pneumonia, a disease to which these animals were peculiarly susceptible and to which most of them succumbed. A few moth-eaten specimens crept south to the desert, it is true, but they were pitifully few and weak representatives of a once numerous and powerful race.

Concl.

36

So there were no more tigers to scare in the paleolithic community, and the best tiger-scaring techniques became only academic exercises, good in themselves, perhaps, but not necessary for tribal security. Yet this danger to the people was lost only to be replaced by another and even greater danger, for with the advancing ice sheet came ferocious glacial bears which were not afraid of fire, which walked the trails by day as well as by night, and which could not be driven away by the most advanced methods developed in the tiger-scaring courses of the schools.

The community was now in a very difficult situation. There was no fish or meat for food, no hides for clothing, and no security from the hairy death that walked the trails day and night. Adjustment to this difficulty had to be made at once if the tribe was not to become extinct.

Fortunately for the tribe, however, there were men in it of the old New-Fist breed, men who had the ability to do and the daring to think. One of them stood by the muddy stream, his stomach contracting with hunger pains, longing for some way to get a fish to eat. Again and again he had

37

tried the old fish-grabbing technique that day, hoping desperately that at last it might work, but now in black despair he finally rejected all that he had learned in the schools and looked about him for some new way to get fish from that stream. There were stout but slender vines hanging from trees along the bank. He pulled them down and began to fasten them together more or less aimlessly. As he worked, the vision of what he might do to satisfy his hunger and that of his crying children back in the cave grew clearer. His black despair lightened a little. He worked more rapidly and intelligently. At last he had it—a net, a crude seine. He called a companion and explained the device. The two men took the net into the water, into pool after pool, and in one hour they caught more fish—intelligent fish in muddy water—than the whole tribe could have caught in a day under the best fish-grabbing conditions.

Another intelligent member of the tribe wandered hungrily through the woods where once the stupid little horses had abounded but where now only the elusive antelope could be seen. He had tried the horse-clubbing technique on the antelope

38

until he was fully convinced of its futility. He knew that one would starve who relied on school learning to get him meat in those woods. Thus it was that he too, like the fish-net inventor, was finally impelled by hunger to new ways. He bent a strong, springy young tree over an antelope trail, hung a noosed vine therefrom, and fastened the whole device in so ingenious a fashion that the passing animal would release a trigger and be snared neatly when the tree jerked upright. By setting a line of these snares, he was able in one night to secure more meat and skins than a dozen horse-clubbers in the old days had secured in a week.

A third tribesman, determined to meet the problem of the ferocious bears, also forgot what he had been taught in school and began to think in direct and radical fashion. Finally, as a result of this thinking, he dug a deep pit in a bear trail, covered it with branches in such a way that a bear would walk out on it unsuspectingly, fall through to the bottom, and remain trapped until the tribesmen could come up and despatch him with sticks and stones at their leisure. The inventor

39

showed his friends how to dig and camouflage other pits until all the trails around the community were furnished with them. Thus the tribe had even more security than before and in addition had the great additional store of meat and skins which they secured from the captured bears.

As the knowledge of these new inventions spread, all the members of the tribe were engaged in familiarizing themselves with the new ways of living. Men worked hard at making fish nets, setting antelope snares, and digging bear pits. The tribe was busy and prosperous.

There were a few thoughtful men who asked questions as they worked. Some of them even criticized the schools.

"These new activities of net-making and operating, snare-setting, and pit-digging are indispensable to modern existence," they said. "Why can't they be taught in school?"

The safe and sober majority had a quick reply to this naïve question. "School!" they snorted derisively. "You aren't in school now. You are out here in the dirt working to preserve the life and happiness of the tribe. What have these practical

40

activities got to do with schools? You're not saying lessons now. You'd better forget your lessons and your academic ideals of fish-grabbing, horse-clubbing, and tiger-scaring if you want to eat, keep warm, and have some measure of security from sudden death."

The radicals persisted a little in their questioning. "Fishnet-making and using, antelope-snare construction and operation, and bear-catching and killing," they pointed out, "require intelligence and skills—things we claim to develop in schools. They are also activities we need to know. Why can't the schools teach them?"

But most of the tribe, and particularly the wise old men who controlled the school, smiled indulgently at this suggestion. "That wouldn't be *education*," they said gently.

"But why wouldn't it be?" asked the radicals.

"Because it would be mere training," explained the old men patiently. "With all the intricate details of fish-grabbing, horse-clubbing, and tiger-scaring—the standard cultural subjects—the school curriculum is too crowded now. We can't add these fads and frills of net-making, antelope-snar-

41

ing, and—of all things—bear-killing. Why, at the very thought, the body of the great New-Fist, founder of our paleolithic educational system, would turn over in its burial cairn. What we need to do is to give our young people a more thorough grounding in the fundamentals. Even the graduates of the secondary schools don't know the art of fish-grabbing in any complete sense nowadays, they swing their horse clubs awkwardly too, and as for the old science of tiger-scaring—well, even the teachers seem to lack the real flair for the subject which we oldsters got in our teens and never forgot."

"But, damn it," exploded one of the radicals, "how can any person with good sense be interested in such useless activities? What is the point of trying to catch fish with the bare hands when it just can't be done any more. How can a boy learn to club horses when there are no horses left to club? And why in hell should children try to scare tigers with fire when the tigers are dead and gone?"

"Don't be foolish," said the wise old men, smiling most kindly smiles. "We don't teach fish-grabbing to grab fish; we teach it to develop a

42

generalized agility which can never be developed by mere training. We don't teach horse-clubbing to club horses; we teach it to develop a generalized strength in the learner which he can never get from so prosaic and specialized a thing as antelope-snare-setting. We don't teach tiger-scaring to scare tigers; we teach it for the purpose of giving that noble courage which carries over into all the affairs of life and which can never come from so base an activity as bear-killing."

All the radicals were silenced by this statement, all except the one who was most radical of all. He felt abashed, it is true, but he was so radical that he made one last protest.

"But—but anyway," he suggested, "you will have to admit that times have changed. Couldn't you please *try* these other more up-to-date activities? Maybe they have *some* educational value after all?"

Even the man's fellow radicals felt that this was going a little too far.

The wise old men were indignant. Their kindly smiles faded. "If you had any education yourself," they said severely, "you would know that the

43

essence of true education is timelessness. It is something that endures through changing conditions like a solid rock standing squarely and firmly in the middle of a raging torrent. You must know that there are some eternal verities, and the saber-tooth curriculum is one of them!"

44

III · THE REAL-TIGER SCHOOL

"THOSE trick mirrors are good," I remarked idly as Dr. Peddiwell and I leaned against the bar rail and surveyed the glittering frames along the wall.

"They <u>distort</u> life," the professor commented judicially.

"But they are funny, and they help to enliven the general *Gestalt* of this place," I pointed out.

"Ah, yes, but they are unreal, artificial," he insisted. "They do not teach us to learn what we live and live what we learn. They have no proper function in a progressive educational institution like this lecture room."

"I didn't know you were a progressive educationist," I murmured.

45

"Well, in one way I am, in another I am not," he replied cautiously.

"What do you mean?" I pressed, knowing that he was on the verge of a lecture. "There is only one kind of progressive education, isn't there?"

"You would not ask so naïve a question, were it not for your lack of historical perspective." His voice took on the accustomed intonation of a first paragraph. "Any careful student of the history of education can tell you that there were progressives and progressives in the past and that the best prediction indicates there will be progressives and progressives in the future. Progressives with new purposes and old machines, progressives with new machines and old purposes, progressives with old machines *and* purposes plus a few new verbalizations to make them less forlorn, and others—others—"

He left his sentence suspended in mid-air and stood gazing at a mirror which magnified his plumpness enormously.

"Was there any progressive education in paleolithic times?" I prompted.

46

"There was the Real-Tiger School, of course," he said absently, still staring at the mirror, "and also—er—the School of Creative Fish-Grabbing. You remember the quarrel that raged between these two progressive institutions, however, and consequently I do not need to—"

"But I *don't* remember," I interrupted. "You never told me."

He tore his gaze from the fat reflection and recovered his usual briskness. "Very good. We are then justified in devoting at least one period to that particular chain of events."

I settled myself and waited for the lecture.

After the new fishnet era was well under way (Dr. Peddiwell began) there was marked dissatisfaction with the traditional school. This dissatisfaction was really directed towards the teachers, for in those days the patrons of the school had the notion that a particular curriculum was really a certain kind of teacher, that a particular system of methods was a certain kind of teacher, and that the whole philosophy of the school was also just a

47

certain kind of teacher. It was a peculiar notion, I admit—unbelievably simple, and all that—but the people had it. Of course they were courteous enough not to *say*, in most cases, that it was the teacher who was at fault. They talked about a better educational philosophy, an improved organization, and all that sort of thing very much as we do today.

By the beginning of the fishnet era, the profession of teaching was pretty well developed, and after the era was well under way, the status and preparation of teachers were rather adequately standardized. In the earlier days of the real-tiger era, teachers had been largely recruited from the ranks of those tribesmen who were too clumsy to grab fish, too weak to club horses, or too timid to face a saber-tooth. By the middle of the fishnet era, this situation had been vastly improved. Teachers were still selected to some extent from the more stupid and less aggressive elements of the population, but any slight disadvantage arising from that condition was more than offset by the new requirements for possession of the teacher's bone.

48

"To learn tiger-scaring, it is quite helpful to have a real tiger."

49

79

The chiefs of the tribe were the ones who made the rules in this regard as they did in any other matters affecting the peace, prosperity, security, and happiness of the people. According to these ✓ rules, every teacher had to carry with him at all times an official bone, usually the thigh bone of an antelope, upon which was scratched the amount of fish-eats' credit he possessed in pedagogy and in one or more of the standard cultural subjects. Since the paleolithic day was divided into periods between the six meals which the tribe liked to have when food was plentiful, and since fish had formed an important part of the diet from time immemorial, the distance from one fish-eat to another came naturally to be regarded as the proper unit for measuring education.

The elementary teacher's bone had to carry at least fifteen fish-eats' credit in special methods of beginning fish-grabbing, the same amount of credit in the methods of teaching elementary horse-clubbing, but only twelve fish-eats for the corresponding methods course in tiger-scaring. Tiger-scaring was a subject which was not offered until the second year of the elementary school, and it

50

was, therefore, recognized as not demanding quite so much preparatory training as the other two subjects. In addition to special methods, the elementary teacher also needed a certificate on his bone that he had earned thirty fish-eats in the theory and practice of paleolithic education.

The secondary teacher's bone requirements were quite different. He had to have only five fish-eats of special methods in each of the cultural fields in which he taught. If he taught only the various branches of horse-clubbing, he needed only a notation on his bone of special methods in that one field. In general theory and practice of paleolithic education on the secondary level, moreover, he needed only twenty-two and one-half fish-eats. The greater surface of his bone had to be covered by notations concerning strictly subject-matter training in his major and minors. The exact number of fish-eats required varied according to the subject. A major in fish-grabbing required forty-five fish-eats, whereas one in horse-clubbing was only thirty-three. This difference arose from the insistence of the professors of ichthyology that secondary-school graduates entered college igno-

51

rant of many of the elements of fish-grabbing. It was therefore necessary, claimed the professors, to devote the first fifteen fish-eats of college work in the subject to teaching what should have been learned in the secondary schools. The professors of equinology, moreover, as soon as they became fully aware of the ichthyologists' success in getting an increase in fish-eats, also protested loudly that they too needed more time for teaching the simplest elements of horse-clubbing to ignorant secondary-school graduates. It was generally conceded by the big chiefs of the tribe, however, that since the ichthyologists had been the first professors to think of making this claim they should be the ones to secure the advantage of extra fish-eats. The equinologists were allotted merely an additional sop of three fish-eats over the standard thirty for college work to quiet their clamor. When the professors of defense engineering, for whose instruction tiger-scaring was a prerequisite, finally awoke to what was going on and made their demand for more fish-eats on the same grounds as their colleagues had cited in the two other fields, the big chiefs rejected the application completely

52

and kept the defense-engineering major at thirty fish-eats.

On the more strictly professional side, professors of paleolithic education gave prospective teachers training in principles and general methods of instruction. These education men faced a very difficult situation from the first. A complete statement of the way in which they fought to overcome their difficulties would be in itself an extensive and important chapter in the history of paleolithic education. It is possible in the time at our disposal merely to outline the main steps in the process whereby the simple subject of pedagogy was transformed into the respectable discipline of education.

In the beginnings of university courses in this field, professors of pedagogy had very little subject matter to teach. They spent most of their time actually trying by precept and example to encourage and direct their students in the work of teaching in elementary and secondary schools. They gave practical hints on the organization and management of classes, described a few rule-of-thumb methods which might be valuable in

53

certain situations, and told stories about the good and bad teachers they had known.

The crude, naïve work of the education professors was regarded with contempt by the subject-matter specialists. It was inevitable that a man who had devoted a lifetime of productive scholarship or systematic speculation to such a problem as The Mystical Element in Sputtering Firebrands as Applied to Tiger-Whiskers or Variations in Thumb-Holds for Grabbing Fish Headed Outward from the Grabber at an Angle of Forty-Five Degrees Plus or Minus Three should be contemptuous of pseudo scholars who were merely trying to show students how to teach.

The academic contempt for pedagogy had a good effect on the education professors. Stung by justified references to their low cultural status, they resolved to make their discipline respectable. With a magnificent display of energy and self-denial, they achieved this goal. First, they organized their subject systematically, breaking it down into respectably small units, erecting barriers to keep professors conventionally isolated from ideas outside their restricted areas, and demanding

54

specialization and more specialization in order to achieve the narrow knowledge and broad ignorance which the paleolithic university demanded of its most truly distinguished faculty members.

Second, they required all members of their group to engage in scientific research in education by counting and measuring quantitatively everything related to education which could be counted and measured. It was here that the professors of education showed the greatest courage and ingenuity. They confronted almost insuperable obstacles in the fact that education dealt with the changing of human minds, a most complex phenomenon. The task of measuring a learning situation involving an unknown number of factors continually modifying each other at unknown rates of speed and with unknown effects was a tremendous one, but the professors did not hesitate to attack it.

Finally, the professors of education worked for academic respectability by making their subject hard to learn. This, too, was a difficult task, but they succeeded admirably by imitating the procedures of their academic colleagues. They organized their subject logically. This necessarily resulted

55

in their giving the abstract and philosophical courses in education first, delaying all practical work in the subject until the student was thoroughly familiar with the accustomed verbalizations of the craft and, thereby, immunized against infection from new ideas. They adopted the
√ lecture method almost exclusively and labored with success to make it an even duller instrument of instruction than it was in the fields of ichthyology, equinology, and defense engineering. They developed a special terminology for their lectures until they were as difficult to understand as any in the strictly cultural fields.

Thus the subject of education became respectable. It had as great a variety of specialists as any field. Some of its professors tried to cover the whole area of the psychology of learning, it is true, but most of them confined their efforts to some more manageable topic like the psychology of learning the preliminary water approach in fish-grabbing. Its research workers were so completely scientific that they could take a large error in the measurement of what they thought maybe was
√ learning in a particular situation and refine it

56

statistically until it seemed to be almost smaller and certainly more respectable than before. Its professors could lecture on modern activity methods of instruction with a scholarly dullness unequalled even by professors of equicephalic anatomy. Their cultured colleagues who had once treated them with contempt were now forced to regard them with suspicious but respectful envy. They had arrived academically.

By the time this goal was reached, however, many of the students whom the professors of education had presumably prepared for teaching were very poor practitioners of the craft. They too tried to be logical, scientific, and respectably dull, and they succeeded in many cases almost as well as their education professors and sometimes even better than their culture professors.

There were a few thoughtful parents of the old New-Fist type who rebelled against this situation.

"But, look here," said the professors of education proudly, "We have succeeded in making our subject academically respectable, haven't we?"

"Why, yes," admitted the radical parents, "but you haven't succeeded in preparing better teachers

57

for the schools. In fact, we are inclined to believe that on some levels of education you have actually made the teaching become steadily worse."

Many of the education professors were intelligent and sensitive men. They squirmed under these charges, and some of them actually began to think about the purposes of education, and a few even went to the length of observing the schools critically. They were struck at once by the artificial character of school learning, by its dissociation from educational objectives, and they set about remedying the situation in various ways.

One group of observers concluded that the chief mistakes in the current educational methods came simply from the circumstance of having too much direction of the learning. "Let the child grow naturally into his learning activities," they advised the teachers. "Let all his purposes and procedures be self-impelled. Without teacher interference or domination, let him always decide what he wants to do, plan what he has purposed, carry out what he has planned, and judge the worth of what he has done."

58

The teachers were disturbed. "But where, then, do we come in?" they inquired. "If the children are going to do it all, they don't need any teachers."

"Oh, no!" assured the experts. "The teacher is a very necessary guide. He will lead the child in the direction of wise choices of right activities and show him how to engage more intelligently and effectively in those activities in which he would have engaged anyway."

"And suppose," said one teacher guardedly, "that a child wants to engage in cutting up fish-nets. Shall I show him how to do it better than he could without my guidance?"

"You are being facetious," smiled the experts. "Get the real progressive spirit and such questions will not occur to you."

Whereupon the teachers withdrew and consulted among themselves. "It is very clear," suggested one, "that we are still supposed to teach fish-grabbing."

"Yes," agreed another, "but we must not tell the children they *have* to learn fish-grabbing. We must just arrange everything so they themselves

59

will think of learning to grab fish and ask us if they can't do it."

"Ah, I see," said a third, "and then we give them permission and guide—guide—"

The teachers then went back to their classes and proceeded enthusiastically upon this new basis.

"Now, children, what would you like to learn today?" one of them began to a class of twelve-year-olds.

The children stared in astonishment. "We're supposed to learn fish-grabbing, aren't we?" they asked.

"Well—er—not unless you *want* to. What do you really *want* to do?"

"I want to leave school and go to work," announced one of the duller boys.

"Ah, but you *have* to go to school," explained the teacher. "Our compulsory education laws, you know—"

"Who is going to decide whether we pass into the next grade in June?" asked a thin, freckled, myopic girl.

"Why—I am, of course," admitted the teacher.

60

The members of the class looked at one another a little dubiously, drew a deep collective breath, and then chanted in polite unison, "We want to learn fish-grabbing!"

"Very well, indeed!" said the beaming teacher. "And how are you going to go about learning fish-grabbing?"

"Don't you know?" asked the pupils accusingly.

"Why, yes, of course, but *you* must plan your project yourself."

"All right, then. If you say we got to do it, why, we got to do it. After all, you're the teacher. Let's get into the water here and start."

So the pupils climbed down into the warm water of the heated school tank in which fish-grabbing had been taught for generations and began to go through the motions they had learned in more elementary classes. The teacher stood on the edge of the tank and shouted guidance to the learners. The children laughed and splashed rather happily and caught the new progressive spirit in good style. They caught no fish, of course, but since they had not been catching fish under the

61

traditional instruction, no one thought anything about it for a while.

For some time the experts were satisfied with the results of the new education. The radical parents were quieted, and everything went along smoothly with the school. At last, however, there was another innovation proposed, this time by a teacher.

One of the boys in the school had been playing truant. When he was caught and brought back to school, his teacher asked him what he had been doing during his absence.

"I was playin'," said the boy sullenly.

"Where were you playing?" asked the teacher.

"Down in the crick."

"What were you playing?"

"I—I don't want to tell."

"You *must* tell."

"Well—I—I was playin' fish-grabbin'."

"*Fish-grabbing!*"

"Yes."

"In the *creek?*"

"Uh-huh."

62

"Well, good gracious! Who ever heard of such a thing! Take off your coat! I could punish mere truancy by having you stay after school, but *this* deserves a whipping. In the *creek!* Indeed! This hurts me worse than it does you, but take that and *that* and THAT! Now you may go to your room."

The teacher might never have made her great theoretical discovery if the punished child had not tried to justify his actions with a final appeal to reason. "Well, my gosh," he sobbed, "the crick is the only place I know where there *is* any fish!"

"That will be enough out of you unless you want another whipping," warned the teacher automatically, but beneath her stern exterior a keen mind was beginning to work at top speed. Forgetful of her surroundings, she paced the floor clenching her fists and breathing audibly through her nose. At length she stopped resolutely and announced her decision. "I will take them down and have them practice fish-grabbing in the creek!"

But when she mentioned this proposal to the school officials, they promptly discharged her. Some of the radical parents were impressed by her vision, however, and suggested that she start a private school for their children—a school of fish-grabbing in a real creek.

The progressive teacher welcomed this opportunity and opened her new school at once. For a while, again, everything went well. The children splashed about in the water happily and the teacher shouted guidance from the bank of the creek.

One day an old independent fisherman who had been absent from the community for many years on an exploring expedition to far-off streams and communities came upon the progressive school in the creek.

"Hello, lady," he said politely to the teacher. "What you got here? A picnic?"

"No, this is a school in session," said the teacher proudly.

"In the *crick?*" asked the old man incredulously.

"Certainly," stated the teacher with some asperity. "It is the Real-Creek School of Fish-Grabbing!"

"That's a good one," laughed the fisherman, "well, so long, I got to be goin'."

"What *is* so funny about it?" demanded the teacher.

64

"Oh, I was just thinkin'."

"About what?"

"Well, if it's fish you want 'em to grab, it looks to me like what you need is a *real-fish* school instead of just a *real-crick* school."

"Real-fish!"

"Yes, ma'am."

"But how in the world—?"

"Say, lady, would you really like to have them kids grab some real fish?"

"Why—I—but you can't—"

"Can't eh? Well, sister, you just watch your Uncle Dudley."

The fisherman threw his pack on the ground and pulled a small length of seine from it. Calling some of the girls in the school to the bank, he gave them instructions. "I'm goin' to get some fish for you kids to play with," he said. "You got to have some place to keep the fish. There's a hole over there about a jump from the water's edge. You girls get some water jars from your mothers and carry water from the crick to fill that hole."

As the girls scurried off to follow these directions, the fisherman told the boys how to help him

65

operate the seine. With intense interest, the children responded to this task challenge. Within an hour the water-filled hole held about fifty jumping fish.

"I don't see what good that will do," said the teacher critically. "Even in that little hole, those fish are too lively to be caught with the bare hands."

*point +
humor*
✓

"Just wait," said the fisherman reassuringly, "watch this." He reached into the water with a stout stick and rapped a fish on the head. Again and again he struck until the surface of the pool was covered with dazed fish moving sluggishly or floating helplessly with bellies upward. "There," he said, "now the kids can do some real fish grabbin'."

With ready insight the teacher caught this suggestion. She marshaled the children at once and set them to work on the activity. With whoops of delight the happy youngsters caught the dopey fish and tossed them ashore. The teacher received the fish and threw them back into the pool as quickly and gently as possible, trying economically to make them last as long as they could be used effectively. When a fish became too inactive and

66

flimsy to serve as part of a real life situation, it was laid aside for school lunch purposes and a fresh substitute was secured from the seining grounds. The teacher rapped the new fish over the heads before they were put in the water. She found that it was easier this way to gauge the force of the blow exactly so that the fish would not be completely stunned but only sufficiently anesthetized to make them slow and dopey in their movements.

The professors of education came and watched this experiment with shining eyes. "Please tell us what is happening here," they begged.

"These pupils are learning what they live and living what they learn," said the teacher.

"But they were doing that in the activity school in which you were first teaching. Now you have them actually grabbing fish. It is wonderful— wonderful—but you've got to explain it with names before we can approve it."

"With *names?* You mean—?"

"We mean *technically.* Now technically, what do you say this is?"

The teacher thought hard. "It is *creative*," she announced finally, "creative fish-grabbing. That's

67

what it is. The children want to grab fish, they plan to grab them, they actually grab them—and right there is the creative part—you see?"

The professors all nodded hard and the most distinguished one even added a "Yes, yes."

"Yes, the children get in there and *create* opportunities to catch fish by grabbing," continued the teacher enthusiastically. "They create the school pool, the school water, and really they create the school fish—well the essence of the whole thing is *creativeness*—you see—and that is why we are going to call this experimental institution the *School of Creative Fish-Grabbing*. The creative part is the heart of the whole movement— just to catch fish—bah!—that's nothing—but to grab fish *creatively*—ah! That is something!"

All the professors nodded again, and the most distinguished one added an "Ah yes."

The concept of real fish-grabbing spread like wildfire. Even the teachers in the school from which the founder of creative fish-grabbing had been fired were forced to give in to a demand for real fish in the classroom. The parents came to them and said, "Our children don't learn to grab

68

fish with the bare hands any more under this present system than they did in the old days. They are impertinent to us at home, moreover, claiming that they must always do as they please in order to develop integrated personalities."

"They *must* have integrated personalities," said the teachers sternly.

"Yes, we know," admitted the parents, "but, for goodness' sakes, get 'em to integrate their personalities around some real fish-grabbing instead of just around raising hell at home."

So the teachers of the school bought some fish, tapped them over the head, put them in the school tank, and started classes in real fish-grabbing.

The director of the creative school sniffed at the whole proceeding. "Huh," she scoffed, "call that tank a *natural* situation! Nonsense! It is artificial! It's too far from the creek. You can't get a *creative* situation except in a natural setting."

The teachers who were thus criticized knew that there was no adequate answer to this indictment. They knew that the situation in their school *was* artificial. The fish in the tank were a long way from the creek. That was the rub. And yet if they

69

tried a hole down by the creek they would be copying the director of the School of Creative Fish-Grabbing, a person who had been discharged from their school.

One day as the principal of the tank school sat gloomily watching the children toss fish around, he was approached by a man who introduced himself as an alumnus of the institution.

"I haven't been back here for twenty years," said the old grad amiably.

"No?" responded the principal, wondering how soon he could get rid of the fellow.

"Yes," continued the alumnus. "I've been trav-eling—away down south—I'm a hunter, you know—"

The principal ceased to listen but just set himself to nodding politely while thinking over the shame of running an uncreative school.

After an interval, however, something in the steady flow of the visitor's conversation began to hammer for attention in the principal's conscious-ness. "Yes, sir," the traveler was saying, "down there in that desert, there are at least two tigers

70

left, maybe more—real saber-tooth tigers—and a man could—"

"What!" cried the principal, as the full educational significance of the statement flashed over him. "What! Actual *living* tigers!"

"Yes, sir. Real honest-to-God tigers."

"Oh, well,"—the principal sank back into his accustomed dejection once more—"it couldn't be done anyway."

"What couldn't be done?" asked the traveler.

"Use these tigers as educational materials. I thought for a minute we might, but now I see it can't be done. We couldn't catch those tigers in the first place, and if we caught them we couldn't make them dopey by just rapping them over the head—probably just make them angry—no, I see it's impossible."

"Well, I don't know about that," said the alumnus aggressively. "I could catch 'em—put 'em in a cage—bring 'em up here. It would cost money, of course, but—"

"Cage!" The principal snapped his fingers, all his gloom vanishing again in a moment. "Cage!

71

Now I see how it can be done. Money? We'll get you the money!"

This was the beginning of the second great institution of progressive paleolithic education. The Real-Tiger School, it was called. Admiring teachers and professors of education came for many days' journeys to see the children of this school line up every morning and wave torches in the faces of two real saber-tooth tigers. The two old tigers, last of their race, toothless, deaf, almost blind, were tired. They asked only to be left in peace in their declining years. They blinked wearily at the children who squealed and waved fire-brands before the cage. They did not like this activity. It was too tiresome for aged tigers.

But the tigers were alone in this attitude. Everybody else liked it. The children had fun. The teachers found the activity stimulating. Even the radical parents had to admit that here was an achievement whose progressiveness could not be denied. The tigers were real and very rare. Their rarity seemed somehow to make their reality all the more meaningful.

72

The general verdict was expressed cleverly and profoundly by the most distinguished education professor. "This Real-Tiger School," he announced, after a thorough investigation, "is the real thing. To the casual observer, these children may appear just to be waving firebrands at a couple of caged tigers, but to me they are *learning* ✓ *what they live and living what they learn!*"

73

IV · HIGHER PALEOLITHIC EDUCATION

"I SEE that the president of the University of Oskaloosa has broken into print again," I remarked.

"What does he appear to have on his young mind now?" asked Dr. Peddiwell.

"He is concerned about the plight of higher education in America," I said.

"And well he might be," remarked the professor approvingly. "Does he say what he is going to do about it?"

"Yes. He is going to make it rational, systematic, orderly."

"Oh, ho! And a very proper thing to try to do, and if he actually did do that, it would certainly be

74

a wholesome lesson to it. How is he going to establish order in higher education?"

"He is going to make the study of metaphysics pervade the whole university. Not information but pure thought is going to be the university's aim."

"A wonderful contribution! Yes, sir—a plan worthy of the best paleolithic thinking and in fact highly reminiscent of the university reform which ushered in the golden age of paleolithic culture."

"Yes, sir?" I breathed softly and waited for the lecture which I could see was on its way.

The paleolithic university, like those of other countries and times (began Dr. Peddiwell), was started for magical reasons. Ordinarily schools gave enough education as long as subjects were taught for their practical values only, but as soon as esoteric knowledge was developed for its own hocus-pocus sake, universities became necessary.

The paleolithic university was really founded the day the paleolithic creek got too muddy for fish to be caught in it with the bare hands. From that time forward, fish-grabbing had to be taught for general cultural or magical reasons, and it was

75

inevitable that the university should be developed for that purpose.

The paleolithic professions of sorcery, chieftainship, and hunting engineering were learned professions requiring university training from the first simply because they were magical professions from the first. The medicine men cast out evil spirits and treated disease, to some extent, by science and common sense but mostly by magic and charm. The chiefs ruled the people, a little by understanding them but a lot by hexing them. Antelope, bears, and fish were caught with snares, traps, and nets in a certain limited sense, but in the more important sense of the supernaturally real, they were caught by prayers and incantations.

Thus professional education and the higher magical education went together in paleolithic times for very good and logical reasons, just as they have gone together ever since. Our young friend, the president of the University of Oskaloosa, is worried by this circumstance. The dear boy lacks historical background, or he would see that any profession which has been saturated with magic throughout its history cannot be divorced from the

76

"Dreading to have illiterate medicine men when our present torch-butt kissers shall lie in the Dust."

77

one educational institution which is devoted to the theory and practice of magic.

The patheolithic university started with a simple enough goal. Because tiger-scaring had once been the most dangerous and dramatic activity in tribal experience, the fundamental passes in the medicine man's ritual were derived from the elementary work in that subject. As tigers became extinct, and the subject of tiger-scaring became purely esoteric, medicine men took over the field entirely. They became the select body of adepts and specialists that the discipline had to have in order to be truly esoteric.

The motto of the university stated the goal quite clearly: *"That we may have smooth tiger-scaring when our present medicine men shall lie in the dust."*

In addition to having a strictly magical purpose, the paleolithic university also had magical subjects. From the very beginning of the university, the value of the education it gave was determined by reference to the magical properties of various subjects rather than by any attempts to

78

discover real changes in students. Thus one subject was considered to give a double dose of magic, while another might give only one-tenth of a dose. Indeed, there were certain subjects which were thought to be anti-magical in their effects.

The whole theory of positive and negative culture arose from these attempts to rate magic dosages in the university. It was not enough for the university to provide positive culture in the way of subjects with approved magic ratings; it must also see to it that no subjects with negative culture values were left lying around where students might be exposed to them.

This system of magic-value ratings for various subjects would have worked much better if the university authorities could only have standardized the dosages. They were unable to do this, however, and the result was an unending struggle between the subject-magic haves and the have-nots.

As we have already seen, tiger-scaring was the first sacred subject. It ruled the university roost for a long time. No one could undertake preparation for any profession without first becoming saturated

79

with the spirit of this discipline, learning all its chants and exorcisms, and mastering all its holy passes and spells.

Perhaps this happy arrangement would have lasted forever, had not the professors of tiger-scaring attempted to advance their subject. If they could only have been satisfied to teach students to go through the sacred motions, all would have been well. As it was, however, although most of the professors were willing to get along with the barest minimum of mental and physical work, there were a few energetic and conscientious professors who created all the difficulty. These hard-working ones knew that professors were supposed to advance their subjects. They knew, furthermore, that a subject like tiger-scaring, which was already considered to be perfect, could not very well be advanced by research. Research looked for new answers; a magical subject already had answers which it was heresy to doubt.

The tiger-scaring professors were forced to do what the professors of any truly holy subject have to do—they had to make greater and greater claims for the magic power of their subject while

80

fighting off the pretensions of lesser subjects to have some magic influence.

So it happened that tiger-scaring, which had once been a useful and relatively simple safety measure and later a kind of moderately magical device for developing general courage in children, became a sovereign remedy for all intellectual and spiritual ills. As nothing else could do, it made men wise and noble and just. It was a touchstone of membership in the tribal elite. It was a guarantee of civic rectitude and private morality alike. It was the subject without which no man could hope to look a difficult fact in the face.

When other professors began to suggest magic claims for their subjects, the tiger-scaring specialists rose to new heights of aggressive reverence for their field. They leaped from claim to claim, rising even higher, until at last they came out flat-footed with the assertion that every detail of the tiger-scaring ritual had been set in the beginning of time by the Great Mystery himself.

At first this claim was pretty generally accepted. Nobody dared to shake his head, be it ever so slightly, at a subject whose claims everybody was

81

required to know and revere. At last, however, the inevitable happened. A professor of ichthyology attacked this newest claim with vigor and courage. He had evidence to support his attack, moreover, and this made the resulting discussion doubly painful in view of the fact that a truly magic subject never requires evidence to support its claims.

The revolting professor had received his appointment by mistake. He had never had the required basic training in tiger-scaring to be a professor of any kind, but through carelessness on the part of the authorities he was allowed to take the most advanced work in general fish-grabbing and the special graduate training in ichthyology. Then, to cap the matter in final absurdity, the man was appointed professor. Of course, a circumstance of this sort could not be kept secret for long. The new professor's colleagues found that he had never secured a single fish-eat in tiger-scaring beyond the secondary level. From that time forward, they paid no attention to his researches, reduced his teaching opportunities to a minimum, and tried their best to keep him from doing

82

too much harm to the good name of the university.

This was the mean and jealous person who started the revolt against the supremacy of tiger-scarers in the university curriculum. He studied the various details of the tiger-scaring routine and finally came forward with sworn statements from a hundred aged tribesmen that the practice of kissing the butt of the torch before beginning the standard tiger-scaring rites had been unknown fifty years before. He produced various other witnesses, moreover, who testified that the practice of torch-butt kissing had been introduced originally by a tiger-scaring assistant at the university who had thought thereby to make symbolic confession of profane love for his landlady's daughter.

The whole paleolithic world was rocked by these charges. The erring professor and the few of his students and colleagues who were tainted at all by his heresy were summarily discharged from the university and forever barred from holding further offices of trust and responsibility. No professors, medicine men, chiefs, or engineers were

83

allowed to take new offices or retain the posts they already had until they subscribed to the following oath; "I do solemnly abjure, detest, and condemn as a deadly error the doctrine that kissing the torch butt was not started by osculation of the Great Mystery himself, and I do solemnly swear that I will oppose this heresy with all my strength and that I will at all times do my utmost to extirpate the root and branch of this and all other errors which are judged by my superiors to be contrary to the theory and practice of tiger-scaring as determined by the paleolithic laws and the regulations of our paleolithic university."

With all these safeguards around the subject of tiger-scaring, it seems incredible that any other subject should ever have been able to attain magic status, but horse-clubbing was fortunate enough to do it in a relatively short time, and fish-grabbing followed soon thereafter. The professors of both these fields followed the standard practice of making stronger and stronger magic claims for their respective subjects until they had developed almost as much reverence for them as had ever been commanded for tiger-scaring in its heyday. The

84

new magic claimants fought each other as much as the older field had ever fought them, moreover, so that each of the three main subjects spent much of its energy in trying to retain as much magic prestige as possible and at the same time keep its two rivals in subordinate positions.

The battle to keep the university curriculum confined to one, two, or a few magical subjects was lost almost before it was well started, however. The followers of one subject could make just as many magic claims for it as could those of another, and it was not long before a large number of subjects were claimed by their supporters to be magically cultural. The only subjects which lacked cultural respectability were those which were studied for their practical effect on the behavier of learners. These subjects remained in a suspected and inferior category, therefore, because they did not pretend to have magic power. Thus the only real disgrace in the university curriculum was seen to be the disgrace of being practical. To modify human behavior for some real purpose kept a subject from becoming truly sacred.

85

√   There were three great reform movements in the history of the paleolithic university. The first reform started with the development of the free-magic system of choosing subjects for the students in place of the original one-magic system which required all learners to go through the same routine. The free-magic arrangement was based on the premise that all approved university subjects were of similar magic virtue. It followed unerringly, therefore, that each student might as well select his own particular dosage. Only the size of the dose was prescribed. Its character was left to free choice. The free-magic system was much appreciated by administrators and professors alike. It helped the administrators by protecting them from the necessity of making decisions about the values of subjects, and it helped the professors by protecting their feelings through assuming that all subjects were equally magical.

    Actually the system of free-magic could not be worked by university professors, and since the details of all university administration were handled by professors, aided by clerks and stenographers who were more professorially minded than

86

the professors themselves, the system broke down of its own administrative weight. By a series of interdepartmental deals, these professors kept modifying the free-magic system until they had an arrangement whereby the only choice a student had was the choice of department. After making that choice he was bound rigidly to follow the departmental magic without deviation. If he selected horse-clubbing, for example, all the power of all the professors, clerks, and stenographers in the department of horse-clubbing was thrown in the direction of making him learn as many details of the horse-clubbing magic as could possibly be forced on him. The professors of other departments, in paleolithic senate meetings, might force some symbolic gesture toward the old free-magic system by requiring fifteen fish-eats for a minor and perhaps as much as twenty fish-eats for free choice, but the sheer weight of ninety-five fish-eats would remain to be devoted exclusively to horse-clubbing and related subjects. If any department did not have ninety-five fish-eats of instruction to offer in its field, the shame of being thus delinquent would soon bring its course offerings up to standard.

87

√ The chief effect of the major-magic system was to make all departments suspicious of one another. The quality of instruction remained just as good as it had been under the free-magic regime or even under the original one-magic system, however. When the goal of instruction was a magical effect, one kind of spell or incantation worked just about as well as another so long as it was applied with the proper faith and fervor.

The third main university reform came with the ushering in of the general-magic system. This was really an attempt to get back to the original one-magic basis without disturbing the devotees of various subjects. It was the result of the old deep-seated yearning for some really powerful educational medicine, something that would be equally good for any one of a variety of ills. One leader suggested tiger-scaring, of course, as the proper basis for showing all students how to think, not what to think.

"Tiger-scaring is the basic discipline," he said. "Every motion of horse-clubbing, every step in fish-grabbing—they all go back to that first activity in tiger-scaring, kissing the torch butt. Do

88

you know any one who is thoroughly grounded in any science or social science who has not been subjected to the mental and emotional discipline involved in kissing that butt? No, you do not. If, in any particular case, you think you do, I can show you quickly enough where the lack of basic education will show up in that case. If it appears nowhere else, it will be bound to show up in an ignorance of the technique of torch-butt kissing."

Other leaders made similar claims for horse-clubbing and fish-grabbing until the great university chiefs decided that all three of these subjects should be called "general-magic" and be given a place of honor in the new university education.

At this point an obscure professor, walking along the creek for recreation one afternoon, fell and hit his head on a rock. His bumps of caution and memory were badly damaged. When he was released from the hospital to return to his university duties, although he appeared superficially to be normal again, he soon gave evidence of the real severity of his head injuries. Freed from the restraint of his usual sense of caution and un-

89

hampered by memory of what a university was like, he began to go around the campus asking questions so naïve as to be practically psychopathic.

"Is a university a kind of school?" he would often begin.

"Yes," his colleagues would tell him pityingly, "A university is a school, an advanced school, a school where the teachers know much more than do the teachers in ordinary schools, but still a kind of a school."

"Schools are educational institutions, aren't they?"

"Of course."

"And is education supposed to change people?"

"Certainly."

"Is it supposed to make them better or worse?"

"Better, naturally."

"Then in order to know what to do with our students in the university, we must discover how to treat them so that they will become better?"

"Well, yes, better, more efficient, more competent intellectually. We must teach them *how* to think, *not what* to think."

90

"A student can become better, more efficient, more intelligent only with respect to the social environment in which he operates?"

"Why—er—yes, I suppose so."

"Then in order to determine what our university curriculum should be, we must first decide what our society should be?"

"Oh, no! Certainly not! That would be the blueprint of a future social order. That would be teaching them *what* to think. Besides, you would be pretending to know what is going to happen tomorrow. Only the Great Mystery knows what is going to happen tomorrow. Are you setting yourself up to be the Great Mystery? You will be lucky not to be struck dead for that impiety!"

"I don't see anything so wrong about attempting to predict what is going to happen tomorrow. If I teach my students tiger-scaring just as university professors have been doing for the Great Mystery knows how many years, will I not, in effect, be predicting that those students are going to be in a society tomorrow in which tiger-scaring will be a very valuable thing for them to know?"

91

"Ah, now you are talking sense," shouted all the professors. "Tiger-scaring *is* good general magic; it is positive culture plus. You stick to tiger-scaring and you'll wear academic diamonds yet."

The questioning professor's head still hurt, but that was partly a result of having hit it pretty hard on a rock.

92

V · EDUCATION AND PALEOLITHIC SECURITY

 "THE American Federation of Teachers is an unprofessional organization," I asserted flatly, taking a firm grip on the bar rail.

"Indeed," commented Dr. Pediwell politely, "and why do you make this statement so vehemently, my young friend?"

"Because I realize the danger to our profession in some of the things which the teachers' union is trying to do."

"One thing, for instance?"

"Well, to ally themselves with labor, for example. That is a shameful thing."

"Ah, *shameful.* A rather severe word, don't you think?"

93

"It is a correct word. They become partisan when they align themselves with any particular group—organized labor! It is terrible. It is unprofessional."

"Ah, yes. Quite, quite. Would you say *un-American* too?"

"Un-American? Well—uh—I don't know—"

"These teachers, you know, they align themselves with all sorts of impossible groups. Some of them are Methodists, some are members of chambers of commerce, and some are even reserve officers. It is all quite unprofessional, I agree, un-American too."

"I—I don't see, Doctor, exactly what—"

"No, you don't see, and the reason you don't see is because you lack historical perspective and background. You look at our present difficulties and fail to see the relationship between them and the task of education. You don't remember how clearly that relationship was developed and ignored in paleolithic times. Why don't you use the lessons of history?"

"Because I don't know the lessons of history," I admitted humbly.

94

"Very well, then," said the professor, "let us find chairs somewhere along this row of lying mirrors, and I shall teach you one of those lessons to the best of my ability."

The paleolithic tribesmen (said Dr. Peddiwell) were cursed with technical intelligence. If they had been somewhat more stupid, they would never have had economic difficulties. As it was, however, their clever inventions of fishnets, antelope snares, and bear pits gave them no end of trouble.

Their chief difficulties came from the ease with which they could make a living under the new system. In the old days practically all the tribe, old and young, had to work hard at grabbing fish, clubbing horses, and scaring tigers. Now, three or four men could catch enough fish in one day to feed the tribe for a week. One man could attend to a whole string of antelope snares which, with relatively little effort, would produce more meat and skins than twenty horse-clubbers could have secured in the same length of time in the old days by the severest labor. A properly constructed bear pit lasted indefinitely, moreover, and after each trail was guarded with one, there was nothing to

95

do but kill the trapped bears and add their great bulk of meat and skins to an already overflowing store.

In time, however, the wise old men of the tribe solved this difficulty. They did it by developing certain rules which they derived from studying the actions of the more clever members of the tribe.

For example, after fishnets had been generally developed and everybody came to use them, it was often very difficult to find a vacant place in the stream to fish. Thus fishing no longer offered merely a technological problem but also a problem in the adjustment of social relations. Indeed it seemed that the more skillful a man learned to be in fishing the harder it was for him to operate without finding his fellows in his way and walking on their toes.

One of the shrewdest fishermen of the tribe, finding himself so crowded by other fishermen that he could not set and draw his net to best advantage, solved the problem by devising a system of ownership of fishing rights. One morning, as the result of unusually good luck the day before, he

96

round that he had five fish more than his family had been able to eat. At first he thought that he would merely take a day off and not fish at all, since five fish would feed his family adequately for the day, but he liked to fish, and the thought of missing the activity for one day saddened him. "How can I get rid of these fish and at the same time get a chance to catch some more?" he asked himself.

As he was thinking over this problem, he watched the fisherman on his right. This man was not a very skillful operator. He set his net clumsily and brought it in too slowly. "I could catch more fish than that man in any hole in the creek," said the clever fisherman to himself. "If I had his hole and mine too, I could catch twice as many fish as I catch now, and probably four times as many as that slow fisherman catches."

So the clever fisherman made the slow fisherman a proposition. "I'll give you these five fish," he offered, "if you will lay off fishing today and let me fish in your section of the creek."

"Well," said the slow fisherman doubtfully, "I don't know for sure whether that's a good bargain.

97

Maybe I could catch ten or twenty fish if I stayed here and worked."

"Yes, maybe you could," said the smart fisherman, "and then, again, maybe you couldn't. Maybe you'd catch only five fish or four, or maybe you'd catch none at all. How many did you catch yesterday?"

"Three."

"Ah, ha! And the day before?"

"Well, it was a bad day, too rainy—I didn't get *any*."

"Ah, *ha!* There you are."

"But the day before *that* I got twelve!"

"Uh-huh, in other words you averaged just five fish a day, just what I propose to give you. You must remember, too, that you worked hard for those fish, and I am going to give you five fish without your doing a lick of work."

The slow fisherman could not count beyond twenty, the number of fingers and toes he had to work with arithmetically, and the process of dividing fifteen by five was altogether too advanced for him, but he was impressed by the mathematical competence of the clever fisherman

98

and by the undeniable fact that he would be *sure* of five fish without any expenditure of care or energy. Because he wanted security more than he wanted to be enterprising and because also he was not very intelligent, he accepted the five fish, told all the tribesmen that his place in the creek was to be held for the day by the smart fisherman, and retired to his cave to sleep away his new-found leisure.

The smart fisherman had very good luck in his double allotment of space. He caught twenty fish more than his family needed to eat. The next day, therefore, he was ready with a new proposition to his slower comrade. "Let me give you a lot of fish," he said, "for the use of your fishing ground always."

"*Always*," repeated the slow fisherman, startled by the proposal. "But what would I *do*? I have to fish somewhere, don't I?"

"No, you don't," the smart fisherman assured him. "All you have to do is to sit and take in the fish I bring to you."

"How many fish will you bring me?"

"I will bring you five fish a day."

99

"Will you do that forever?"

"Well, practically forever. I'll bring you five fish every day until I have brought you ten times ten times ten fish. You can see yourself that it will take a very long time to pay up a debt like that at the rate of five fish a day. In the meantime you can snare antelopes or trap bears the same as anybody else. You'll be rich, for you can have as much meat and skins as anybody for your work and in addition you will have five fish a day rolling in without your ever having even so much as to lift your hand."

To one of the slow fisherman's limited mathematical competence, *ten times ten times ten* sounded like a quantity of the order that the French war debt would sound to the average citizen today. All the slow fisherman could see ahead of him when he listened to those figures was a rosy security stretching far into the future. He accepted the proposal with alacrity, therefore, and the chief of the tribe was called in to scratch a statement of the bargain on the sacred bone which was used for that purpose.

100

The clever fisherman was so successful with his catches that within a few days he felt able to make similar arrangements with another slow fisherman. Finding that he prospered on this venture too, he soon had the rights to half a dozen fishing holes. The fish tended to crowd away from the more heavily fished part of the stream into the relatively quiet territory of the smart fisherman's six-man stretch of water. He was consequently able to catch ten times as many fish in six holes as he had before caught in one.

In less than seven months the smart fisherman had paid completely for the first individual fishing right he had bought, and before the end of the year he had finished paying for six and had contracted to buy ten more. Two of the remaining fishermen who were clever enough to see the advantages of private ownership and energetic enough to seize those advantages began to follow the same procedure. At the end of very few years the fishing industry was owned and operated by three great fish chiefs.

The fishermen who sold their stream rights were able to work for a while in the antelope and bear

101

industries, but they crowded the trails so much that the process of developing private ownership of hunting rights was thereby hastened. Again the slower, more stupid, more luckless, mathematically more inept tribesmen accepted a temporary combination of security and leisure and turned over their trail rights to a few aggressive, energetic, lucky, and clever men who built up the antelope and bear industries as the fish chiefs had built up the fishing industry.

Of course the three great fish chiefs soon came to the place in the expansion of their activities where they were unable, even with the help of all members of their families, to keep all their nets in operation. They began to hire propertyless men to operate their nets and smoke their fish. They paid an adult worker two fish a day. When it was pointed out to them that the average family had to have five fish a day barely to exist, the chiefs replied that the average family had two adults and three children, that the two adults could earn four fish a day, and that the children however small and weak ought to be able to do half the work of an adult and thus earn the remaining fish needed for the family sustenance.

This arrangement was actually possible for a few families in the earlier stages of the development of the industry. For a while the great fish chiefs hired all the help they could get, men, women, children. They kept the nets working even at night on some occasions. The great chiefs sat on the bank of the stream, paid out wages, and watched the steadily growing pile of smoked fish.

After this boom had gone on a little time, however, the fish chiefs had great difficulty in getting rid of their wealth of fish. Sometimes they traded a few fish for antelope and bear hides, sometimes they gave a lot of fish for bear-tooth necklaces wherewith to adorn their wives and daughters, but still their fish piles grew and grew. They had to catch fewer fish. They reduced the amount of their fishing, throwing their workers out of jobs. The men who remained on their pay rolls were attempting to feed five-fish-per-day families on two fish. The unemployed ate no fish at all but tried to subsist on berries or an occasional bite of antelope or bear meat.

103

The wise old men who were the main chiefs of the tribe saw that something would have to be done, so they made a rule that any fish chief who would give the whole tribe a pile of fish as high as a man might buy the exclusive right to make fishnets in his neighborhood. All three fish chiefs immediately accepted this offer and turned over their piles of fish to the tribal government. The government began to give one-half fish a day to every man who was unemployed and one-quarter of a fish for every woman and child he had in his family. Thus a family of two adults and three children which needed five fish to live on in the old days and which recently had tried to get along on two fish, now tried to get along on one and one-half fish. The fish chiefs, on the other hand, were now entirely safe in the control of the industry. The tools of production as well as the places in which to fish were entirely in their hands.

The antelope and bear chiefs were impressed with the success of the fish chiefs, so they went to the great rulers of the tribe and asked very respectfully, "Do not the laws which you wise old men

104

make apply everywhere to everybody with equal force?"

The old men took counsel with one another and then answered solemnly, "It is true that the laws which we make are universal. It is an essential mark of wisdom to know much more than any single case can show. We are wise. We made these laws. Therefore they are universal. They apply to any case. Incidentally, if it is of interest to you, they are eternal too."

"Good," said the smooth antelope-snarers and bear-pit-watchers. "We know now how to become great chiefs and really develop our industries. We shall compete with one another in free and open business."

"May the best men win," said the rulers.

Thus the antelope and bear industries were developed along the lines which had been laid down in the fishing industry. The piles of fish, meat, and skins grew higher and higher, and the long lines of unemployed waiting for their tribal ration became bigger and bigger.

The stores of fish, meat, and skins became so large, however, that the great industrial chiefs

105

could not find any use for them. They loaned fish and meat, they rented skins, always for the price of more fish, meat, and skins, and so finally they had to close down their industries altogether and wait for the accumulated piles of wealth to rot.

Now everyone was out of work, and everyone except the few great fish, antelope, and bear chiefs were out of food too. The tribal authorities used up their small store of relief provisions very quickly. The unemployed tribesmen wandered idly up and down the creek staring hungrily at the rich stores of food and covering. Wild-eyed radicals climbed upon rocks and began to make inflammatory speeches. The poor people listened to these stupid and insane statements until they were actually ready to rush the piles of food and skins and take by force what they needed for themselves and their families to eat and wear. The situation was desperate, as all the clever tribal rulers and industrial chiefs could readily see.

The rulers were equal to this emergency, however. They called all the chiefs into consultation and taxed them as follows. Every fish chief had to

106

pay the tribal authorities one fish out of every hundred he caught. All persons who ate fish, moreover, had to give the tribal authorities two hundredths of a fish for every fish they ate. Similar taxes were levied on antelope and bear meat and skins. With the food and covering thus secured, the tribal government was enabled to resume relief to the unemployed. A great economic crisis was thus averted.

One day a demented tribesman got upon a rock by the creek bed and addressed his fellows in the following words. "The whole trouble with our economic system lies in those original rules which were figured out by some smart boys at the expense of some dumb boys and then adopted by the chiefs just because the smart boys belonged to their gang. Let's change those rules," he suggested.

"How would you change them?" asked some of his hearers.

"Let's just use our common sense and put everybody back to work on fishing, antelope-snaring, and bear-pit digging and watching," said the orator. "Maybe there are some other things that could be found for us to do. Anyway, let's all get

107

to work and let's all eat and wear whatever we can get."

His hearers looked at each other wonderingly. They knew there was something very bad in this man's suggestions, but at first they couldn't figure out what it really was.

The Daughters of Barehanded Fish-Grabbers, the members of the Loyal Order of Stuffed-Horse Clubs, and the Sons of Saber-Tooth Veterans heard of the man's statements, however. They came and listened to him. They saw what was wrong with him and his proposal, and they knew immediately how to handle him.

"You are preaching an un-paleolithic ism," they said to the demented worker. When he persisted, they warned him, "Shut up or we will duck you in the creek."

Most of the man's hearers now saw plainly what was wrong with him and his argument. "We see through you now," they shouted. "Shut up or we will duck you in the creek."

"I stand on my rights as a paleolithic tribesman," began the worker, "and I am merely telling you what I think would be a good and wise and

108

expedient thing to do. Is it a crime for me to tell you that?"

Then he started to repeat his suggestions for improving the life of the tribe, but when he came to the place where he actually came right out and proposed that the rules of the wise old men should be changed, the good citizens standing there grabbed him and ducked him and held him under water until he promised faithfully to behave himself in the future.

A teacher who had been standing in the crowd and observing this exciting event asked his fellow teachers about it next morning. "In education shouldn't we do something definite, have something clearly in mind, have a particular goal which will modify the behavior of our people so that they can arrange some system of hunting and fishing that will keep them better from starvation?"

"We can teach them *how* to think, *not what* to think," chanted his fellow teachers in unison.

"But we have plenty of fish, meat, and skins for everybody to have enough to eat and wear if they only knew enough to eat and wear them," insisted the inquiring teacher. "Surely we teachers can

109

help the people to educate themselves sufficiently to attain such a simple goal as that."

Whereupon his fellow teachers hung their heads and kicked their toes in the sand embarrassedly. Finally the oldest and wisest teacher of the lot spoke the sentiment of the whole group.

"You'd better not repeat that in any of your classes," he said warningly. "You'll get your neck out too *far*—you'll get your ears slapped *down*—you'll get *fired*, that's what *you'll* get. School teachers are not supposed to change people's ways so much that the people will change the rules of the wise old men, and don't you forget that. Don't you forget *that*, just as long as the wise old men run the schools, or the first thing you know you'll be on the outside looking in."

The inquiring teacher thereupon hung *his* head, dug *his* toes in the sand, and resolved to mend his ways. He kept his resolution faithfully, and as a result he was not fired until the economic difficulty in which the tribe found itself became so grave that all schools had to run on half the number of fish they had been granted in the past.

110

VI · THE PALEOLITHIC YOUTH PROBLEM

"THE youth commission has got out a new report," I announced, handing a copy of the article to Dr. Peddiwell.

"Ah, yes," he murmured, without looking at the report, "it is indeed a sad situation, a sad situation."

"What do you mean, a *sad situation?*" I demanded.

"Ah, yes," he continued placidly, "a sad situation and one not susceptible to treatment by modern educators."

"What do you mean, *not susceptible to treatment by educators?*"

"When the average educator finally, after due deliberation, heart searchings, and conferences

111

with the president of the First National Bank and the secretary of the Chamber of Commerce, decides that it would be all right, proper, educationally correct, to try to get over a wall which seems to be in the road of progress, he always attempts to make a nice little ladder by which he may crawl over the wall cautiously."

"Well, what's wrong with that?"

"Nothing is wrong with it, except that we need a lot of educators who can at least recognize that there are other ways of getting over that wall."

"What way, for instance?"

"We need educators who will see the possibility occasionally of getting some nice big sticks of dynamite, planting them in neat holes at the base of the wall, producing a spark at the right moment, and blowing the whole works to—er—small pieces."

"But I don't see—"

"Of course you don't see, and the reason why you don't is because you lack historical background, the background that gives perspective. You look at our present youth problem and the

various ingenious proposals for its solution, and
you forget that the problem was equally distressing
in paleolithic days and was solved in equally
ingenious fashions."

"Yes, I do forget. Go ahead, Professor."

With this introduction and stimulus, Dr. Peddiwell settled himself in his chair, took a firm grip
on his glass, and launched into the following
lecture.

During the depression caused by having too
much fish, meat, and skins, the paleolithic youth
problem was very acute. It was hard enough for
the older members of the tribe to secure work in
the fish, antelope and bear industries, but the
young adults had no chance for work at all. After
studying the fundamentals of fish-grabbing, horse-
clubbing, and tiger-scaring in the elementary
schools, the young people went into the secondary
schools and took advanced work in the same
subjects, until at about the age of eighteen it was
thought best for them to finish their secondary
education. They all wanted to go to the paleolithic
university and learn to become medicine men,
chiefs, and engineers, but most of them could

113

never hope to secure the necessary fish, meat, and skins to pay for this higher education. Many of those who did go to the university found it difficult to get places in their professions after they were graduated.

A few young people tried to make a living by sneaking out at night and stealing fish from the nets or meat from the snares of the great chiefs, but this was a very dangerous practice. The great majority were too honest to do anything of this sort. They wandered idly about, getting the necessary minimum of food and skins from their parents or from the relief grants allotted to them by the wise rulers of the tribe.

A temporary occupation for the young adults was found in a pile of smooth pebbles and rocks ranging in size from marbles to bowling balls. This rock pile was up on the hill back of the tribal caves. Some of the more energetic young people began to go up to the rock pile every day and play various games with the stones there. Other young men and women who had completed their formal education and who were unemployed soon followed. It was not long before most of the

114

"Is it possible that they are just monkeying with those rocks?"

115

young adults of the tribe knew how to amuse themselves on the youth rock pile, and some of them were quite adept at it.

Various games were played at the rock pile. Some young people played marbles with pebbles, others used somewhat larger stones for a kind of billiard game on the ground, and still others used the largest stones for bowling balls. Certain of the less athletic young persons with an eye for form and color arranged various piles of rocks according to their shapes and tints or made patterns and designs in rock walls and borders.

More and more youths came up the hill to play with rocks as more and more games were invented to utilize them. Even some of the older unemployed people, finding time heavy on their hands, followed the young people up the hill and adopted this method of using their leisure. At times the rock pile was so crowded that players had to take turns in order to get the use of even a small rock.

Occasionally a few of the more dangerously discontented young people would flare up in resentment at what appeared to them to be the purposelessness and uselessness of their activities. Some of them even had the temerity to say, "We have a right to work for ourselves and our tribe. Are we to be kept forever in this baby play with rocks? This was the sort of thing the children of the tribe were doing ages ago when the great and wise New-Fist saw them and invented the first educational system to give them something useful to do, to prepare them for *work*. What this tribe needs is not more leisure but more work. Some of it can be truly recreational work, but none of it should be this degrading busy-ness with play designed merely to keep us from thinking too much about our difficulties. Let us take a bunch of these stones down the hill and use them to break the antiquated rules of the medicine men! Maybe, before we get through, we can use some of these rocks to break a few heads! Maybe that's the way to get some action on the changed ways this tribe needs!"

Most of the persons on the youth rock pile were good paleolithics of the best boy- and girl-trapper type, however. They reported these cases of unrest to the medicine men and assured the authorities

117

that they knew they could get nowhere by being radical in the slightest degree.

The wise rulers of the tribe saw the possibility of danger, nevertheless, and resolved to take steps well in advance to solve the youth problem before it became too embarrassing. After considering various ways in which they might acquire the necessary information and skill to deal with the problem, they decided to use the method of a general conference. They had great faith in the conference method of attaining wisdom and developing techniques. So they began by appointing a paleolithic youth commission and calling it into immediate session.

The members of the youth commission represented all the most important elements in the tribe. The fish, antelope, and bear chiefs sent hired men to act as their mouthpieces. Some of the greatest professors of fish-grabbing, horse-clubbing, and tiger-scaring were there. The federated brotherhoods of fishnet, antelope-snare, and bear-pit workers were represented by their great president who had done so much to keep them contented with the rules of the medicine men. The

118

young people themselves, of course, were not represented by any of their number, as it was well understood that every member of the commission considered himself a representative of the youth of the realm.

The commission members suggested several solutions of the youth problem.

One of the professors, a man who knew more about fish-grabbing-with-the-bare-hands than any other man in the paleolithic world, made a plea for the continued education of youth. "Let us put these young people back in school," he said. "Although they have studied elementary and advanced fish-grabbing, most of them have been very poorly taught. I get them in my freshmen classes in the university, and I know how ignorant they are. They have only the vaguest notions of how a fish should be grabbed with the bare hands. There is available in the journal and monograph literature of this subject a great mass of data which could be organized and taught to these young people in a good, stiff two- or three-year course on the junior college level, along with, possibly, some of the less important subjects. Thus when these

119

unemployed youths get old enough to acquire jobs and family responsibilities, they will possess the trained minds and hands which only the thorough study of fish-grabbing can give them."

Professors of other subjects agreed with this report in part, although they insisted that more advanced courses in horse-clubbing and tiger-scaring were even better designed than fish-grabbing to develop the strength and courage which the young people would need so badly when and if they finally got jobs.

The industrial leaders had a very different proposal. The fish chiefs' leading hired man suggested that all workers over fifty years of age should be retired and their places should be filled by young men taken from the youth rock pile. "In the fishing industry, for example," he explained, "these older people now receive an average wage of two fish per day. Although they get slower in their work with advancing age, moreover, their powerful and arrogant labor leaders threaten to tie up the whole industry with a strike if we reduce these wages. If they are retired under a tribal pension scheme, the tribe can pay them an allow-

120

ance of one-half fish per day and the fishing industry can hire young people to replace them at one
fish per day. Thus unemployment will be mate-
rially reduced, the youth problem will be solved,
and the whole realm will benefit because the
fishing industry will be prosperous."

At this juncture the door of the conference room
was flung open and a small group of young men
and women burst into the room. After some argument their spokesman, a wild-eyed, hungry-look-
ing boy, was allowed to present the views of the
young people themselves.

"In spite of all the big piles of smoked fish, dried
meat, and tanned skins down there by the creek,"
he said, "there are many members of this tribe who
don't have enough to eat or wear. Our caves are
crowded, ugly, and insanitary. There is hardly
sleeping space in many of them; they are full of
bugs and lice and filth. We have no pictures on
the walls of our caves. We sit glumly by the fire
at night with never a song or a story to express our
emotions and lighten the dull load of living for
food and shelter alone. We need many things
which we do not now have and which we could

121

easily get if we were only permitted by the rules to work for them. We need more and better food, skins, shelter, songs, stories, and pictures.

"There is much work to be done, and we young people are ready and eager to do it. We can dig bigger and more convenient caves, we can learn how to cut down trees and make beautiful dwellings of wood such as the tribe over the mountains builds but which we have never enjoyed. We can make broad and smooth pathways back into the deep forest where other animals than antelopes live, and we can devise traps for those animals, thus improving and varying our food supply. We can compose songs and stories to delight the whole tribe. We can make pictures on the cave walls to show ourselves and the Great Mystery that we men are something more than the beasts who merely live, eat, drink, fight, reproduce their kind, and die. We are tired of playing with those damn' rocks up on the hill! Let us work, we beg of you wise old men, and we will increase the tribe's store of welfare and happiness more than enough to pay you for giving us this boon of labor."

122

The commission members were aghast at this radical proposal. They saw clearly that the poor boy who spoke did not understand the rules of the medicine men. They felt sorry about his ignorance and the ignorance of his little, misguided group of followers. But there was obviously only one thing to do, and so at a given signal from the presiding medicine man, the entire commission rose and with one accord threw the young people from the conference room. Then they sent an unofficial message to the Loyal Order of Stuffed-Horse Clubs, asking that the order should undertake immediately an investigation of un-paleolithic tendencies in the schools. As one of the medicine men said in an executive session of the commission, "We feel sure that these young people must have come under the tutelage of certain teachers who have thought about something more than educational matters of fish-grabbing, horse-clubbing, and tiger-scaring. A teacher who would do that is un-paleolithic to the core!"

After this disturbance was over, the commission settled down again to serious work and finally solved the youth problem. They organized a

123

153

√ special administration to handle the problem. The administration sent out scouts to all the neighboring valleys and hills to search out new and bigger rock piles. As soon as discovery of a rock pile was made, experts were sent to classify and arrange the rocks for convenient play. Other experts were set to work devising rules for new games that could be played with rocks. Rock-play administrators and supervisors were appointed to organize and direct the work. A survey of all available youth was made with careful tabulation of individual and group preferences for big rocks and little rocks, gray rocks and red rocks, smooth rocks and rough rocks, round rocks and irregularly shaped rocks. Data were assembled and treated statistically, plans were drawn up, appropriations from the tribal fish and meat piles were made, and before long the greatest rock-pile movement in paleolithic history was well under way.

One day when the rock-pile players were busily engaged in their leisure-time activities under the direction of a corps of experts, a strange figure was seen to appear over the brow of the hill above the rock pile and watch the scene below him for a long

124

time. At length one of the rock-pile supervisors became curious and climbed the slope to examine the stranger at close range.

"Greetings, friend," he called as he crawled over the last boulder that separated him from the solitary watcher.

The stranger raised his hand in the usual gesture of amity but said nothing. This taciturnity together with the fact that he was dressed in skins of an unfamiliar sort made him appear very foreign indeed. The rock-pile supervisor continued the friendly overture with some constraint in his manner. "I see you are watching our leisure-time program," he said politely, "and I wonder if I can help you in any way—give you information about our work—take you down to observe it in detail—anything—?"

"You call it a leisure-time program?" asked the stranger abruptly.

"Yes."

"What is leisure time?"

"Why—ah—it is the time you have when you don't have to work."

125

"Oh. I am looking for education. I thought this was some kind of an educational program."

"Well, in a way, it is."

"An educational program without work?"

"Yes."

"And with rocks?"

"Yes. They learn with rocks."

"*What* do they learn to do with rocks?"

"Well, they *play*—recreation, you know."

The stranger's eyes shifted ominously, and his hand tightened on the shaft of his hunting club. "They learn to *fight* with those rocks," he said flatly.

"Oh, no," protested the shocked supervisor, "not at all! Just recreation, I assure you."

"What's *recreation?*"

"Why—er—don't you *know?*"

"No."

"Don't you have a recreation program in your tribe?"

"No."

"Well, let me see, recreation is what you do to make a better life after you get through making a living."

126

"Oh. When do those young people down there work for a living?"

"Well, right now we have a lot of unemployment, you see, and these particular young people don't work. They have never worked."

"Never?"

"No, never. They have never had any jobs."

At this point the stranger showed clearly that he lacked manners. He stared hard at the rock-pile supervisor for much longer than the socially approved maximum. Then he turned without a word further and started back over the brow of the hill toward the hinterland whence he had come.

"A good journey to you!" the supervisor called in courteous farewell.

The stranger nodded grimly over his shoulder, struck a smart blow with his hunting club at a wayside boulder, and then dropped out of sight down the trail.

VII · THE DISINTEGRATION OF DR. PEDDIWELL

IT WAS a gray morning for Tijuana, and the professor appeared distrait. The comic mirrors along the wall might as well have been nonexistent for all the attention he gave them. The long stretch of bar appeared no longer to have philosophical meaning for him. He slumped in his chair at the table and toyed apathetically with his daisy glass. I tried one line of attack after another in a vain effort to find the adequate stimulus for a lecture, but finally I fell silent too. It must have been that a premonition of disaster was slowing my cerebral processes. I know that something gave my daisy a faint bouquet of castor oil. That must have been a subjective phenomenon, for Luis was a most careful bartender.

At last the professor himself broke the ice. "Do you know what lecture this is?" he asked dully.

"What lecture?" I repeated, stupid with surprise.

"It is the *sixth* lecture, the *last* lecture, in fact it is the lecture after the lecture that *should* have been the last lecture."

"Sixth? *Should* have been last?"

"You remember I had only five days to spend on this course? The time is up. It was really up yesterday. I gave myself one day extra, but now the absolute deadline approaches."

Now I knew the reason for Dr. Peddiwell's strange manner. I had lost track of the days, of course, but his keen time sense had checked them off like a navigator's chronometer.

"Do you *have* to leave today, Doctor?" I asked miserably.

"Yes," said the great man resolutely. "I have to go—tonight. Tomorrow morning, according to the itinerary carefully arranged for me by Mrs. Peddiwell who attends faithfully to the details of all my journeys lest I get disconcerted by the way, I

129

must appear in San Diego fresh from my scholarly labors in the north—er—was it Palo Alto, Stanford, where I have been working?"

"No, sir. Berkeley. At least you told me that you were working in the library this week at the University of California."

"Quite right, sir. And that is where it was, or rather where *I* was, or am, until tonight when I shall take a train south and arrive at San Diego in the morning to greet the little woman and escort her back to Petaluma. The final sessions of the League of American Needlewomen will be—er—pulled off, I think the phrase is, tonight in a blaze of oratory, and Mrs. Peddiwell must hasten to retail to the Petaluma chapter of the organization all those lessons she has learned at the national convention while they are still fresh in her memory."

"Ah, well," I said consolingly, pretending to a courage I did not feel. "There will be other times. We'll come back to Tijuana again. Once more you will lecture before this longest of all long bars in the world. Once more we shall—"

"No," interrupted the professor firmly. "It is not to be."

"But surely you can—surely Mrs. Peddiwell will permit you to arrange—surely she will attend another convention some—"

"Oh, yes, no doubt." He brushed the question of his wife's future whereabouts to one side as though it were of less than no consequence to him. "But that is not the prime issue. The prime issue is this." He lowered his voice almost to a conspiratorial whisper. "*Today's lecture is really the last one because it deals with the last of the material.*"

"You mean—?"

"I mean I am at the end of my knowledge of the paleolithic field. Beyond this point my researches do not go. I have tried this morning, but after I go a little ways I come to a veil which I cannot penetrate. Perhaps another scholar—more gifted— more industrious—more sensitive to daisies— might hope to go somewhat further—but for me, it is finished!"

His manner was so sure, so impressive in its humility, that I could not say a word. I merely sat in silence and waited for the summarizing statement which I hoped would come.

131

I have tried to see what was happening in the valley of the tribe on the other side of the mountain (Dr. Peddiwell began hesitantly), the tribe to which the strange observer of rock-pile recreation belonged, but it has been hard to get very much. I have had some success, it is true, but the details are not very clear. The general import is unmistakable, however.

This strange tribe had a single ruler. He was a practical man who had little interest in magic or culture. His shoulders bulged with hard muscles as he swung his heavy club. His brow was lined with the deep marks of an habitually fierce scowl. His massive chin jutted aggressively at any men or events that attempted to stand even momentarily against his will. When he spoke, he always shouted in rhythmic, guttural grunt-patterns which had powerful hypnotic effects on his people. Under the stimulus of his grunts and example, they too shouted rhythmically, waved their clubs fiercely, and stamped in unison until the ground trembled beneath their heavy tread.

The ultramontane tribe was not troubled with unemployment. All the men and boys who could

132

possibly be spared from hunting and fishing were put to work for the tribe by the ruler. They gathered rocks as did the recreation group on the other side of the hill, but instead of playing with the rocks they made weapons of them. Some stones they selected for hand missiles, others they put aside for use in slings, and still others they shaped into axes which they bound to stout handles.

Only half of the working day of this group was spent in making weapons, however. The remaining daylight hours were devoted to practice in the use of these weapons. The first result of this specialization in weapons was a very effective system of hunting. Fewer and fewer men were needed to supply the tribe with food and clothing, and more and more men could be assigned to the tasks of making and learning to use weapons. The second result was that as the members of the tribe developed skill in the use of weapons they developed also an intense and growing desire to employ the weapons in war against some other tribe.

The scowling ruler talked of various reasons why the tribe might well go to war. He spoke of tribal destiny, of tribal honor, and of tribal need

133

for achievement of bloody ends, but most of all he spoke of inferior peoples who must have their ways changed with clubs. The real reason that he and the tribe desired war, however, was to use their weapons and to secure a wealth of meat and skins by fighting rather than by work of a more prosaic kind. Like other men, they did not commonly speak of their real reason for the action they were going to follow.

The tribe had really reached a peak in potential fighting skill. The ruler recognized that fact and was beginning to be worried about it. He knew that there was danger of overtraining his men if he drilled them much longer without having them fight somebody. He could not continue to scowl and grunt forever about future military glories; he had to have an actual battle or two to talk about. Moreover, he was getting a little weary of his own speeches. He yearned for action so intensely that his clubbing muscles ached.

The ruler was delighted, therefore, when his comparative-education scout returned and reported the state of affairs in the community over the mountain.

134

"But don't those people have rocks?" the ruler asked.

"Oh, yes, Your Bigness," answered the scout, "but they do not really use them—at least not for any purpose of importance."

"Don't use them! What the hell do you mean?"

"Well, they monkey with the rocks in various ways, but they don't do anything with them for the good of the tribe."

"But how can they get the tribe's work done that way? Are you trying to be funny with me, you crawling worm?"

"No, no, Great One. I have never a thought for anything but the sober truth. I know that what I say sounds unbelievable, but I am giving you as true a picture as I know how to give. Those people over there don't have any notion of what they want the tribe to become."

"Don't they have any education to give them a notion?"

"No, Bigness, not in the sense of an activity planned to put the tribe nearer to any clear-cut goal. They do have something they *call* education, but it is just a collection of traditional activities,

135

a machine which they worship for its own sake. The result is pitiful. They have plenty of meat to eat and skins to wear, but they are so uneducated that they don't know how to distribute food and covering, and consequently many of them are wretchedly fed and clothed. They have a tremendous amount of work to do, yet they are so uneducated that they force many of their people to be idle all the time. They are forever blocked in attempts to better their lives by reason of having only mis-education, pseudo education, in place of real education."

The great ruler's scowl deepened. "Good," he muttered. "Such a people need to be taken over by a superior race. We march at dawn. See that the necessary orders are given now."

Dr. Peddiwell fell into silence again. I waited for him to go on with the story, but he continued to stare moodily at his glass without a word.

"And *did* they march?" I finally ventured.

"They did," he answered shortly.

"And how did the war come out?" I persisted.

136

"What would you think?" asked the professor. "I have given you the background. I have told you how New-Fist's tribe started with a system of purposeful education and how that education was degenerated through the years into a system of red-tape, magical culture. Use your imagination, my friend. I have used mine until it is exhausted. I have to start for San Diego."

"*Start for San Diego*," repeated a voice so grim that it could hardly be called feminine though it came undoubtedly from some kind of a woman. The professor whirled in his chair as though in response to the crack of a rifle and then slumped back as though the bullet had hit him between the eyes. I looked up and remained frozen by what I saw standing behind him.

In the ten years since I had seen her, Mrs. Peddiwell had grown somewhat grayer, somewhat broader, but her characteristic unpleasantness of manner had not changed a whit so far as I could judge.

"Start for San Diego?" she repeated harshly, stepping forward in order to glare down more

137

readily at her husband's stricken countenance "And why, may I ask, J. Abner Peddiwell, do you happen to be starting from *here?*"

The professor did not attempt to answer, and probably his wife did not expect him to answer, for she went on swiftly in the same merciless tone. "Here in a *saloon!* With a dirty bum!" She eyed me momentarily, but with obvious disfavor. "And what's this? Are you *drinking?* Have you actually been drinking *liquor?*" She snatched up his half-filled daisy glass, held it briefly to her nostrils, and then smashed it viciously on the table top. The crash brought both of us automatically to our feet.

Luis dashed through a bar portal and came running forward with a towel and an agonized expression. Dr. Peddiwell handed him a twenty-peso note and spoke in brief farewell. "Good-by, Luis," he murmured quietly. "I am going away. No more daisies, Luis, ever."

"You weel come back, Senor," Luis assured him sympathetically. Before the professor could answer, his wife had caught his arm in a powerful

138

grip and was propelling him rapidly toward the door.

I am proud of what I did then. Although the mere sight of that woman paralyzed me, I fought off my terror and rushed forward to grasp the professor's free hand. "Thank you for the lectures, Doctor," I said chokingly. "I can never repay you!"

"Don't mention it, my friend," he replied politely. No circumstance, however terrifying, could take from him his sure sense of proper courtesy. Then, with a faint smile as he was being dragged through the door, he added, *"But my chronology must have been off by one day!"*

139

A Historical Note on This Book and its Author

In reviewing the thirty-year history of this remarkable little book, one cannot fail to notice several interesting oddities, of which at least one seems to be attributable only to the hand of the Great Mystery fatefully at work in the publishing world.

First, the book was published without benefit of a contract of any sort between the possessor of the manuscript and the publisher — an almost unheard of thing in book publishing practice of that or any other day.

Second, copies of its first printing were given away, not sold — a senseless thing, certainly, when viewed in retrospect.

Third, its publication was opposed by the only editor in McGraw-Hill who was professionally qualified to judge its merit and acceptability — which suggests that too much specialized knowledge can be a dangerous thing in a book editor.

Fourth, in view of that editor's opposition, it was first offered with much fear on the part of the publisher, but none at all in the heart of the possessor of the manuscript. He could, and often did, deny that he was the author.

Fifth, like New Fist's primal techniques of fish-grabbing, horse-clubbing, and tiger-scaring, the book's great initial popularity faded in time, only to be revived strongly when new generations of students and teachers discovered that its verities were both timeless and universal. This enduring popularity was greatly enhanced, by the way, twenty years after publication when the book was made available as a modern classic in a paperback edition and at a price of one and one-half fish rather than four fish. Students then, even as in the saber-tooth days, were always short of fish, it seems.

Finally, comes now the event where the hand of the Great Mystery is the most clearly revealed — namely, the publication of this Memorial Edition of *The Saber-Tooth Curriculum* under an agreement whereby the royalties and profits derived from its sale will go at last into a fund for the support of teacher education. More, later, about this long-delayed fulfillment of the author's wish.

The history of *The Saber-Tooth Curriculum* as a published work can be briefly told.

The manuscript was submitted, as I remember, to our College Department editor who was then, in 1938, working with Harold Benjamin, the consulting editor of the newly established *McGraw-Hill Series in Education*. It was presented with the author's usual air of modest diffidence — with an apology, almost, for bothering us with such a trifling work. The editor, a fairly recent liberal arts graduate of Harvard, liked the manuscript and gleefully recommended publication. It had come, he said, like a breath of fresh air blowing over his desk.

But where would this unusual book fit into the McGraw-Hill departmentalized lists? Not, certainly, into the college-level series of texts and reference books. Then perhaps the School Book Department should handle it. So the manuscript was turned over to our school book editor, the one who had the better credentials for judging it. He was a Ph.D. from Columbia's Teachers College with several years of professional experience in research and teaching. He, too, liked the manuscript, but it left him full of fear of its possible ill effect on the reputation of the McGraw-Hill imprint. Would sober-sided educators appreciate the sharp satire and the merciless caricatures of several prototypes of their kind? And what about the shocking anomaly of a nice professor of education being found in a hellhole like Tijuana, bellied up to the longest bar in the world, soaking up tequila daisies, a deceiving fugitive from his good wife's company? And, even worse, what about those slyly symbolized low-language references to such vulgar matters as the techniques of advanced butt-kissing? Gad, just imagine how some people would react to our publishing stuff like that!

Well, in the end this editorial dilemma was solved, as most dilemmas are, by a compromise. It was decided that *The Saber-Tooth Curriculum* would be published as a stunt, in a clearly tongue-in-cheek way, which would allow a cautious testing of reader reaction.

The sales manager of our School Book Department was instrumental in this canny editorial decision. He, too, was a liberal arts graduate of Harvard, a man of brilliant wit and a great reconteur. His *soirées* at meetings of educators were famous, and those at the annual NEA conventions were always jam-packed and joyous affairs. He had devised and scored great success with a very cleverly simulated honorary degree of *Doctor Conventium* (awarded by the "Universitas Hardis Knockorum"), which he had conferred with mock ceremony and high fun on most of the prominent educators of the day. Since that stunt had begun to wear a little thin at Atlantic City and elsewhere, he shrewdly seized the idea of *The Saber-Tooth Curriculum* as something new and different and equally droll for McGraw-Hill's next *chef-d'oeuvre*. Harold Benjamin thought it was a dandy idea, so it was agreed that the work would be printed in a small edition (2,000 copies) and tested as a giveaway souvenir at the forthcoming winter meeting of the Department of Superintendents of the NEA.

The appearance in print of the lectures of J. Abner Peddiwell did not, of course, surprise those of Harold Benjamin's friends (including me) who had heard him deliver many bits and pieces of Peddiwell's hilarious profundities at intimate and often late-hour social gatherings. But it did surprise most of the educators who were selected to receive copies at the NEA meeting. They had never heard of J. Abner Peddiwell, of course, and apparently most of them had never dreamed that their sedate profession could be lampooned in such an outlandishly funny but intellectually scorching way. Nevertheless, the book was received with quick word-of-mouth approval that built up to a roar of delight by the end of the convention. The last of the 1,000 copies that had been taken to Atlantic City were given away well before the McGraw-Hill "reps" had folded their stand and started their weary way back to New York. What a great hit that little book had made! Harold Benjamin was quick to express his own pleasure, but with continued diffidence. He expressed some surprise, even, but one could tell that he was not really surprised at all. Obviously, he knew his fellow educators, and what was in their hearts and minds, far better than his publisher did.

After the NEA meeting, our School Book Department was immediately flooded with requests for additional gifts of *The Saber-Tooth Curriculum*. The second 1,000 copies of the first printing quickly disappeared, and still the requests flowed in—and, mark you, never a murmur was heard about the questions that had so much bothered our School Book editor. Hence it was easy to decide that the book should be reprinted and sold at a modest price. This was done, as noted earlier, with only an oral agreement on royalty payments and other rights and conditions of the business transaction.

The first three printings of the "commercial" edition were sold within a short period and with considerable excitement and satisfaction all around. J. Abner Peddiwell soon became nationally known, and his lectures were widely cited and quoted by educators young and old. *The Saber-Tooth Curriculum* was assigned reading for courses everywhere. Yet, naturally, both the excitement over the book and its sales rate diminished in time to levels where the demand was just sufficient to justify modest reprints (averaging 1,000 copies) every second or third year. Nevertheless, eleven printings were made within the book's first twenty years; it held on with remarkable, but not very profitable, durability. It simply refused to be forgotten and buried as books of its kind usually are after a few years of flashy life.

In 1959, twenty years after its publication, *The Saber-Tooth Curriculum* was selected with several other of McGraw-Hill's more durable backlist titles for reprint in a new "quality" paperback series—a series produced primarily for sale on college campuses. The first printing was 5,000 copies; the price was $1.50 as compared with the then current price of $3.90 for the clothbound edition. Given wide exposure at the lower price in college bookstores, the paperback edition went like hotcakes. It has since been reprinted fourteen times, and over 100,000 copies have been sold in the past ten years. A remarkable record, certainly, for a book first printed more than thirty years ago with caution and with more than a little misgiving. The revivifying and sustained success of the paperback edition gave the author a great deal of quiet satisfaction in his later years. Unhappily, he did not live to see the publication of a French-language translation thirty-one years after the first publication of the English edition—which was, of itself, a most unusual event in the publishing world.

I first met Harold Benjamin in 1930 when he was associate professor of education and director of practice teaching at Stanford University. I was at the time a youngish college traveler for McGraw-Hill, and as such I was scouring the Stanford campus two or three times a year, promoting adoptions and looking for new authors. I had been befriended, fortunately, by Prof. Lewis M. Terman, a great teacher and scholar and a very kind man. He told me that Harold Benjamin was a brilliant teacher and writer and lent me a copy of his *Introduction to Human Problems*, published that year by Houghton Mifflin. I liked the book very much, and "Uncle Lewis" (as he was called by Harold and several other of his bright young protégés at Stanford) made a point of introducing the two of us when I next visited the campus.

I immediately liked the author as much as I had liked his book. Clearly he had a good mind with a strong philosophical bent. He was a ravenous reader of all kinds of books. He was full of folk wisdom and was a great teller of folk tales. His manner was direct, alert, and friendly with a warm, homespun quality. His wit was sly and lively. He was as far removed from pedantry in mode and mind as any college professor I had ever met.

Moreover, Harold and I soon found that we had many common interests and partialities. Both of us loved the Far West and life in the great open spaces. Both of us had worked on ranches earlier in life—he as a real-life occupational cowhand, I as a summertime tenderfoot. Both of us knew and liked the Mexican border country, and both of us had some imperfect "gringo" Spanish, in which we delighted to chatter. He loved the academic life, and I had (at the time) a strong yearning for it. He had plans for the writing of many, many books, and I had plans for publishing all of them at McGraw-Hill. Small wonder that we quickly established a close and enduring friendship.

Having the same surname and being both of us associated with McGraw-Hill, Harold and I were at times mistaken by strangers as being one and the same person. More often we were mistaken as brothers, or at least as cousins. Naturally, and hopefully, we examined early in our friendship the question of a possible family relationship, but we found no evidence of collateral descent among our known progenitors. Yet we were convinced that there surely must have been, somehow and somewhere, an early family connection of some sort. We settled the matter by deciding that, in any case, we were certainly "spiritual" cousins. And since each of us was called "Ben" by his professional and business associates, we soon fell into the habit of addressing each other as "Cousin" Harold and "Cousin" Curtis.

This personal account of an old friendship is related here largely to indicate why we in McGraw-Hill turned to Harold Benjamin when we decided in 1935 to expand our comparatively small list of college texts and professional books on education. It took some persuasion to gain his agreement to become our consulting editor. He had become by then an assistant dean and director of the Center for Continuation Study at the University of Minnesota. His heart was in his new administrative work, and he was teaching a few stimulating courses on the side. Moreover, he was not sure that he had the ranges of knowledge, and personal acquaintance that our job required. He argued, with his customary modesty, that we should find an older and more experienced person, someone with a reputation much wider and higher than his.

On the other hand, his interest in books, in their writing and editing, weighed heavily on our side. And there was another highly tempting consideration: the thought that quite possibly the McGraw-Hill editorship might in time earn enough in royalties to allow Harold Benjamin to do something as grand as, or even grander than, "Dad" Cubberley had just done at Stanford — which was to give $550,000 for a new building to house the School of Education. Everyone knew that that munificent gift had been made possible by wise investments of royalties that Cubberley had earned as long-time editor of the *Riverside Series in Education* published by Houghton Mifflin—a series that had dominated its field for many years but had by then started on a downward slide. There was no good reason, I argued, why Harold Benjamin could not repeat the Cubberley performance for a noble purpose of his own. This prospect appealed so powerfully and irresistibly to Harold's nature that he finally accepted our proposal and plunged immediately into planning the new series, which was announced in 1936.

Over the next twenty years almost one hundred titles were published in the series, all save a few of which were reviewed, edited, and introduced to the reader by Harold Benjamin. (The exceptions were a few titles published early in the World War II years when Harold Hand, a close friend at Stanford, served briefly and very competently as substitute editor.) So successful was the series that it did, in fact, soon succeed to the dominant position that had been so long enjoyed by the older Cubberley series. Indeed, I think it can be safely said that the Benjamin series was one of the most successful of all the many academic series of its kind ever published in America.

Further, I think it can be safely claimed that the series served to heighten the quality of both the academic substance and the literary style of pedagogic books in general. In exercising his editorial stewardship, Harold worked hardest at trying to improve the directness, the lucidity, the liveliness, and the general readability of his authors' styles. He was an unrelenting foe of the jargon, the circumlocutions, and the pretentious pedantic trappings that had long characterized the style of pedagogic books. And certainly he himself led the way in his crusade. He adopted the then unusual practice of contributing an editor's introduction to each book published in the series. All of these contributions were lively, perceptive, and provocative as well as informative. Some of them were polished gems, and even the hastily written ones had the sure stamp of the editor's free mind and engaging style. Indeed, there were in some cases lamentable stylistic contrasts between the editor's introduction and the author's text that followed.

The foregoing encomium is not intended to suggest that Harold Benjamin was the perfect editor, for that he certainly was not. Often his reviews of manuscripts were slow in coming in. Now and then his failure to supply an introduction on schedule would delay a book's publication while the author and the publisher fretted impatiently. Yet he always came through with something that caused the delay to be forgiven and forgotten. And he always had good excuses, because Harold Benjamin, like all other men of genius, had a reach for perfect performance that ever exceeded his grasp. In any case, the liveliness, intelligence, and sagacity of his correspondence and reports were a never-failing source of delight to those of us in McGraw-Hill who were on the receiving end.

But the source's flow was interrupted during World War II, when Harold was faithfully back in his other career as a soldier and officer in the U.S. Air Force. Witness the following excerpt from a letter which I wrote to his wife, Georgia, in 1943 when Harold was serving in the Aleutians: "In these dismal days we miss Harold's sparkling reports on manuscripts and manuscript proposals. As you know, Harold Hand carried on in fine style for a while, but we have now lost his services also. We despair of finding another acceptable substitute so we have decided to continue a more or less passive development of the series without benefit of an editor for the duration of the war. Meanwhile, we shall long for Harold's return."

After the war Harold stepped back into his editorial harness with eagerness to make up for lost time, and for several years the series prospered mightily. But as the years went by, he became more and more interested and involved in the affairs of international education. Increasingly he was called upon to undertake, in addition to his teaching load, a number of foreign missions and studies, some of which took large chunks of his time and energy. At the same time, the McGraw-Hill education series, having grown to almost 200 titles, was demanding increased care and feeding. It all added up to a work load that was clearly beyond the scope and power of even a superman of Academe. A solution to the McGraw-Hill side of the problem was found by dividing the large series into four smaller intradisciplinary series, with associate editors appointed to take over direct responsibility for three of them. Harold himself continued to be responsible for the subseries called the Foundation Series, and he continued a lively avuncular interest in the other subseries as well.

Having spoken of the pleasure which Harold Benjamin's reports and letters gave us through the years, I should add a word about the striking impressions of his personal visits to our offices in New York City. He came in (often unexpected and unannounced) as fresh and refreshing as a summertime breeze off the western slope of the Rockies. With courtly manners and a large hat in hand, he would address receptionists and secretaries and female copy editors with the politest of "Ma'ms" — obviously he considered them to be people deserving of much respect. He would be equally respectful and friendly in greeting other editors, young and old, with whom he had business to transact. But when he got down to the business in hand, his manner would be direct, outspoken, unequivocal, and even blunt if need be. The business done, he would relax and ask permission to roll his own cigarette from a packet of papers and a sack of Bull Durham that were always in his shirt pocket. He could, and often did, perform this uncommon feat with one hand, the while glancing up slyly to observe the effect of his performance. This was, I always thought, one of the most artful and delightful affectations that I ever saw in any man.

But the thing about Harold that most impressed our citified people at McGraw-Hill was, I think, his clear, steady, leveling way of looking at the person with whom he was talking. I knew it to be the look of a man who had lived long in the Far West, who had looked long across its deserts, over its plains, up at its mountains. Some of my associates did not know exactly how to take such a direct, riveting look, but it seemed to help all of them to understand that they were dealing with a man of unusual intensity, intelligence, and integrity. To the end and wherever he went, Harold Benjamin carried with him his Western manner, speech, and folk wisdom. He was always an attractive visitor, and his friends at McGraw-Hill wished that he would come back to see us more often.

It should be recorded here, and for a good purpose, that the editorial royalty earned annually for the account of Harold R.W. Benjamin was quite substantial for many years. Yet little of it was saved, and none of it was placed in long-term investments of the kind that had made possible "Dad" Cubberley's handsome gift to Stanford. Alas, that fond aspiration was never to be realized. It was simply because Harold generously gave away his money, as he did his personal kindness, to the needy as he went along. A friend who knew him well has said, "Ben was above all else generous. Nobody will ever know the names of all the struggling students whom he helped with gifts of cash when they needed it; both he and Mrs. Benjamin preferred to be reticent about the sums they gave away. In addition to personal gifts, they gave a number of fellowships here and there, including the Charles Knudsen Fellowship for doctoral students in education at Peabody."

The foregoing remark now brings me back, at the end, to one of the oddities that was described at the outset. This is the fact that thirty years and more after publication of *The Saber-Tooth Curriculum*, the desire concerning payments of royalty expressed by Raymond Wayne—the self-assured young man who allegedly first presented the manuscript to Harold Benjamin—will at last be honored.

The reader will recall that that flashily dressed but dimly seen young man said that he wanted royalties on the book, such as they might be, to be spent "for giving professors of education some basic training in methods of teaching." Well, the production of this Memorial Edition fulfills the young man's longstanding stipulation: All royalty and all profit earned on its sale will go into a fund for establishing at the University of Maryland a distinguished professorship to be named in lasting honor of Harold Raymond Wayne Benjamin, the greatest New-Fist of his time. Who, then, can fail to see that the hand of the Great Mystery still works fatefully and well for our friend who has gone "to the Land of the Sunset far down the creek"?

Curtis G. Benjamin
formerly President and Chairman
McGraw-Hill Book Company
director and consultant, McGraw-Hill, Inc.

Under His Own Command:
The Careers of Harold R. W. Benjamin

Many glimpsed him for a first and only time as an unforgettable conference keynoter or commencement speaker. Lean and rangy, blue-eyed and boyish, dignified yet somehow warmly familiar, he suddenly stood tall behind the lectern. His infectious charisma easily evoked laughter and solemnity and always inspiration. He lifted audiences by his magic, made multitudes of teachers proud of their profession, chided antiquated ideas with humor, moved even cynics, and touched all with rare insight and a moral note that sank deep.

He told a graduating class of teachers in 1966: "I long thought that intellectual ability was a prime indicator of later professional achievement. Without being anti-intellectual, I now doubt that concept. Watch two waitresses at a busy lunch room: one muddled, inaccurate, slow, surly; the other keeping myriad details straight and serving with smiling, sprightly grace. The difference is in one's driving spirit, craftsman's pride, and search for high achievement, regardless of the work. Or to use the more descriptive Sioux Indian word, the difference is in one's *wakan*."

His adventurous beginnings were believable when one saw him expertly roll a Bull Durham cigarette, or lean against a tree in cowboy boots chatting with students, or watched his loping stride. The son of Harriet Louise Locke Benjamin and banker-farmer-logger-rancher Herbert Samuel Benjamin, Harold Benjamin was born in Gilmanton, Wisconsin on March 27, 1893, and grew up in Salem, Oregon, where the family moved in 1904. He grew up on the open range. Campfires and big sky, the smell of leather and the feel of horses, and contact with Sioux Indian Chief Medicine Horse, his first teacher, are nostalgically recalled in his slightly disguised autobiography, *The Sage of Petaluma*. After graduating from Tualatin Academy, Forest Grove, in 1910, he homesteaded with his father and a brother in Alberta, Canada. He returned to study at the Oregon Normal School in Monmouth, and in 1915 began his educational career as teacher and principal in the one-room, rural Salem Heights Elementary School. Some mixture of adventurous patriotism led him in 1916 to join "Blackjack" Pershing on the Mexican border in pursuit of Pancho Villa. When world events transferred Pershing to France to lead the American Expeditionary Force, Sergeant Benjamin of the horse cavalry left the Mexican border for Oregon, where he enlisted as Private Benjamin. Years later during the McCarthy era, when rightists attacked American education, Harold Benjamin, speaking publicly in defense of academic freedom, was interrupted by a challenge to his patriotism. Continuing amid strained silence, Benjamin casually mentioned action he had seen in Belleau Wood and the Black Forest and his battlefield promotion to lieutenant. "And what battles were you in, sir?" he asked. No answer. When the speech ended, the audience stood and shook the hall with applause.

On August 26, 1919, Benjamin married his long-time fiancée Georgia Kessi, whose wise counsel and devoted support were important in his career. (She was a housewife and mother of three when she earned a Ph.D. degree at Stanford in 1928, and Harold Benjamin used to say that he was probably the only husband who typed his wife's dissertation.) Busy early career years followed as Superintendent of Schools in Umatilla, Oregon (1920–22); editor of the weekly Umatilla *Spokesman*, (1921–22), and student at the University of Oregon (B.A. 1921 and M.A. 1924, and serving as Assistant Professor of Education (1922–25).

At Stanford University he was a teaching fellow from 1925 to 1927, earned the Ph.D. in 1927, was Director of Practice Teaching from 1927 to 1931, and served as Associate Professor of Education and Psychology from 1928 to 1931. He left for the University of Minnesota to become Professor of Education and Assistant Dean, College of Education, (1931–36), Director of the Center for Continuation Study, (1936–37), and Minnesota Director of Adult Education, (1933–34 and 1936–37). Then, at the University of Colorado, he was Professor of Education and Psychology, Director of the College of Education, and Dean of the Summer Quarter, (1937–39).

Richly experienced and nationally respected as teacher, administrator, speaker, writer, and editor, in 1939 he moved across country to serve as Dean of the University of Maryland's College of Education and Dean of its summer session, a post he held until 1951.

When war came again, he interrupted the Maryland years to volunteer at age 49, eschewing a deskbound colonelcy for field action as a captain. He declined the offer of a tour in the European theater for new experiences and hard missions as a combat intelligence officer in the Aleutian Islands, (1942–44) and the Philippines, (1945). His postwar assignments were with the Command and General Staff College (September 1947); the General Staff, Department of the Army (September 1948); and the Army Field Forces Board on the Education of Regular Army Officers (November 1948 to January 1949). He was the only civilian member of that board. He was for many years an Air Force Reserve lieutenant colonel. Though he detested war as education's major enemy, and though he spoke little of his personal war exploits, he always included his military record in biographical accounts. *Under Their Own Command*, his Kappa Delta Pi lecture containing probably his most penetrating educational ideas, is resoundingly antiwar.

He entered the arena of postwar rebuilding, a natural step for one whose comparative and international education interests dated from research he did in England in 1921 for his dissertation. He was tapped for important missions: technical adviser to the U.S. delegation at the constitutional conference of UNESCO in London (1945); U.S. member (1946) of the Education Committee of UNESCO's Preparatory Commission(where was written the lofty preamble, "Since wars begin in the minds of men, it is in the minds of men that the defenses of peace must be constructed"); organizer and first Director of the International Education Division, U.S. Office of Education (1946); and a key member of important education missions to Japan in 1946 and 1950, Afghanistan in 1949, and South Korea in 1954–55. Yearning to use education for international understanding and peace, he developed what was then something new in higher education, the University of Maryland's University College of Continuing Education, with strong overseas branches to bring broader vision to American men serving the free world.

Wanting more time for classroom teaching, he became in 1951 Professor of Education and Divisional Chairman of Educational Foundations at George Peabody College for Teachers. His work in South Korea enabled Peabody College to strengthen teacher education in that country under a $7 million U.S. aid contract. An esteemed Peabody colleague, Prof. Clifton L. Hall (now retired), recalled, "Ben and I settled most divisional questions in less than ten minutes each, he sitting on the corner of my desk or I on his. . . .I came to appreciate his ability to drive directly to the heart of an issue, state it in a few plain Anglo-Saxon words, and arrive at a commonsense solution."

Colleagues and students—they all became his friends—remember the warmth of his home, his guitar playing and ballad singing (he wrote many of the songs himself). They also remember his wife's charm as a hostess and the striking interests of their talented daughter and two sons—all the family played musical instruments.

Harold Benjamin retired from his Peabody College post in 1958, but he remained productive and in demand during his eleven post-retirement years. He was Visiting Professor of Comparative Education at the University of Buenos Aires, Argentina (1959–60); Chief Consultant on Education, Comparative Study of Higher Education in the American Republics, Rio de Janiero, Brazil (1960–62), one result of which was his book *Higher Education in the American Republics* (1965); Distinguished Service Professor of Education at both Glassboro State College (1962–63 and 1966) and Southern Illinois University (1963–64); EDUCARE Distinguished Professor of Education, University of Southern California (1965); and Professor and Assistant to the Dean, College of Education, University of North Dakota (1967).

Honorary degrees came from Drake University in 1955, Pacific University in 1962, Rhode Island University in 1965, and both Glassboro State College and the University of Maryland in 1967. He was listed in *Who's Who in America* continuously from 1942 and was a member of Phi Beta Kappa. Long associated with Kappa Delta Pi, the national honor society for men and women in education, he was elected to its Laureate Chapter on March 29, 1949. He established and chaired Kappa Delta Pi's International Education Commission; anonymously donated its early international fellowships, which were later named the Harold R. W. Benjamin Fellowship in International Education; and was the Commission's Laureate Counselor from 1952 to 1958.

Some consider *Under Their Own Command* to be Harold Benjamin's richest educational work. Yet his widest and perhaps lasting renown rests on *The Saber-Tooth Curriculum* over which two generations of readers have chuckled. To a reporter's inquiry about the number of his books, he hesitated, never having kept precise records; he estimated that he had written about 15 books or conference reports, coauthored some 16 other works, and edited and written introductions to some 126 texts and professional books in the McGraw-Hill Book Company Education Series. Colleagues often remarked on his sure touch in identifying needed textbooks and potential authors.

After a fall in August 1968, he wrote characteristically to a friend from his hospital bed, "I was astonished to see how much of a big deal the physicians and neurosurgeons made of a simple rap on the head." That Christmas at home when he found himself unable to dial the telephone he knew it was time to return to the hospital. He died Sunday night, January 12, 1969, at University of Maryland Hospital in Baltimore, eleven weeks before his seventy-sixth birthday. Besides his two sons and a daughter, he left seven grandchildren, two great grandchildren, and a brother since deceased.

At the funeral service in the University of Maryland Chapel, College Park, Vice-President R. Lee Hornbake said: "We shall miss Dr. Benjamin's imagination, his contemporary outlook, his leadership, his humor, his courtly charm. Most of all we shall miss his inspiration for justice and fairness, for the right of everyone to become the best person he can become."

A Peabody College colleague, Clifton L. Hall, wrote: "Something went out of American education that will not soon be restored. . . .He was an uncompromising fighter for the things he believed in. . . .No really important educational gathering seemed complete without Ben. . . .[His] erudition, rich experience, wit and warm human sympathies are precious things rarely found."

His own *wakan*, a supreme faith in the lifting power of education, he expressed in military terms in *Under Their Own Command*:

> Whatever the difficulties before us. . .there will be education reaching out and conquering more and more of the behavior changing patterns of the world for the benefit of all the peoples of the world. . . .Let us resolve that if we win this engagement, we will win magnificently and that if we fail, we will go down striking shrewd and daring blows. . .until all the peoples of this planet can move forward in peace and happiness under the command of their own hearts.

Those to whom he was a stranger may but pause briefly in closing this book. Those who knew him well may blink a time or two for the rare Ben who is no more. Then, recalling his boyish verve, they will be glad for the remembrance of this uplifting man, who was a teacher most assuredly under his own command.

Franklin Parker
Benedum Professor of Education
College of Human Resources
and Education
West Virginia University
at Morgantown

A Bibliography Compiled by Franklin Parker

The Harold R. W. Benjamin papers are deposited in the Library of Congress, Washington, D.C. A productive scholar and busy lecturer almost to the last, Dr. Benjamin disdained keeping an up-to-date curriculum vitae, thus challenging his bibliographers, later ones of whom will undoubtedly record elusive works not listed here. A collection of some of the best of his writings and speeches is in Robert M. Bruker (ed.), *Wakan: The Spirit of Harold Benjamin: A Collection of the Writings of Harold R. W. Benjamin* (Minneapolis, Minn.: Burgess Publishing Company, 1968, 247 pp.). The following chronological bibliography consists of Books and a Serial Issue either written or edited by Benjamin (not including the extensive McGraw-Hill Book Company Education Series), Articles in Serials and Books, Obituaries, Unpublished Manuscripts and Speeches, and Addenda.

Books and a Serial Issue

1. *An Introduction to Human Problems* (School Edition). Boston: Houghton Mifflin Company, 1930. 450 pp. Reprinted as *Man, the Problem Solver* (Trade Edition). Boston: Houghton Mifflin Company, 1930. 472 pp.
2. (Coeditor), *Modern School Administration*. Boston: Houghton Mifflin Company, 1933.
3. (Coeditor), *The Historical Approach to Methods of Teaching the Social Studies*. Philadelphia: McKinley Publishing Company, 1935.
4. (Editor), *Education for Social Control, Annals of the American Academy of Political and Social Science*, CLXXXII (1935). 242 pp.
5. (With faculty of the Standford University School of Education), *The Challenge of Education*. New York: McGraw-Hill Book Company, 1937. 471 pp.
6. (Coeditor), *Capitalizing Intelligence*. Cambridge, Mass: Harvard University Press, 1937.
7. *Community Forces and the School*. Washington, D.C.: National Education Association, 1939.
8. *The Saber-Tooth Curriculum*. New York: McGraw-Hill Book Company, 1939. 139 pp.
9. (Coeditor), *Learning the Ways of Democracy*. Washington, D.C.: Educational Policies Commission, 1940.
10. *Emergent Conceptions of the School Administrator's Task* (Stanford University School of Education Cubberley Lecture, 1938). Stanford, Calif.: Stanford University Press, 1942. 26 pp.

11. *Under Their Own Command: Observations on the Nature of a People's Education for War and Peace* (Kappa Delta Pi Lecture Series). New York: The Macmillan Company, 1947. 88 pp.
12. *The Cultivation of Idiosyncrasy* (Inglis Lecture, 1949). Cambridge, Mass.: Harvard University Press, 1949. 37 pp.
13. (Editor), *Democracy in the Administration of Higher Education* (Tenth Yearbook of the John Dewey Society). New York: Harper & Brothers, 1950. 240 pp.
14. *True Faith and Allegiance*. Washington, D.C.: National Education Association, 1950.
15. (Coauthor), *American Education Faces the World Crisis*. Washington, D.C.: American Council on Education, 1950.
16. (Coauthor), *Report of the Mission to Afghanistan*. Paris: UNESCO, 1952.
17. (Coeditor), *Forces Affecting American Education*. Washington, D.C.: National Education Association, 1953.
18. *Building a National System of Education* (in Korean language), 1955.
19. *Higher Education in the American Republics*. New York: McGraw-Hill Book Company, 1965. 224 pp.
20. *The Sage of Petaluma: Autobiography of a Teacher*. New York: McGraw-Hill Book Company, 1965. 233 pp.

Articles in Serials and Books

21. "Type of South American University Revolution," *School and Society*, XX, no. 514 (Nov. 1, 1924), pp. 557–559.
22. "Some Initial Difficulties in Work of Inexperienced Teachers of Modern Languages," *Modern Language Forum*, XV (January 1930), pp. 7–8.
23. "Administrator and Student Morale," *American School Board Journal*, LXXX (June 1930), p. 46.
24. "Red Tape in Education," *American School Board Journal*, LXXXI (October 1930), p. 48.
25. "Fable of Guidance," *Minnesota Journal of Education*, XII (May 1932), pp. 333–334.
26. "National Teachers College of Copenhagen," *School and Society*, XXXVI (Nov. 26, 1932), pp. 699–700.
27. "Age and Sex Differences in the Toy Preferences of Young Children," *Pedagogical Seminary and Journal of Genetic Psychology*, XLI (December 1932), pp. 417–429.
28. "European Plan for Educational Reform in China," *School and Society*, XXXVI (Dec. 17, 1932), pp. 789–791.
29. "Ellwood Patterson Cubberley, A Biographical Sketch," pp. 349–377, in John Conrad Almack (ed.), *Modern School Administra-*

tion: Its Problems and Progress. Boston: Houghton Mifflin Company, 1933.

30. "Five Year Curriculum for Prospective Secondary School Teachers," *Educational Administration and Supervision,* XIX (January 1933), pp. 1–6.
31. "Nature of Curricular Problems," *Education,* LV (November 1934), pp. 163–165.
32. "Education in Mexico's Six-Year Plan," *School and Society,* XL (Nov. 17, 1934), pp. 666–668.
33. "Course of Study Revision as a Teaching Procedure in the Small High School," *Junior-Senior High School Clearing House,* IX (December 1934), pp. 229–231.
34. "Social Reconstruction and Method," pp. 1–8, in *Historical Approach to Methods of Teaching the Social Studies.* Philadelphia: McKinley Publishing Company, 1935.
35. "Cultural Attaches for Chilean Legations," *School and Society,* XLI (Mar. 9, 1935), p. 339.
36. "Education and National Recovery in Denmark," *Annals of the American Academy of Political and Social Science,* CLXXXII (November 1935), pp. 173–180.
37. "Revolutionary Education in Mexico," *Annals of the American Academy of Political and Social Science,* CLXXXII (November 1935), pp. 181–189.
38. "Community Studies Recently Sponsored by State Departments of Education," abstract on pp. 8–9, in *Reconstructing Education through Research: Official Report.* Washington, D.C.: AERA, 1936.
39. (Editor's page), *Child Study,* XIII (February 1936), p. 129.
40. "Reform of Secondary Education in Argentina," *School Life,* XXI (June 1936), pp. 287–288.
41. "Center for Continuation Study at the University of Minnesota," pp. 107–111, in *National University Extension Association Proceedings,* XXII. Bloomington: Indiana University Extension Division, 1937.
42. "Residential College for Adults," *Harvard Education Review,* VII (January 1937), pp. 52–56. Condensed in *Education Digest,* II (March 1937), pp. 63–64.
43. "Center for Continuation Study," *Journal of Adult Education,* IX (April 1937), pp. 151–154.
44. "University's Unique Experiment," *Adult Education Bulletin,* I (April 1937), pp. 8–10.
45. "Mexico Sows New Seeds," *Nation's Schools,* XIX (April 1937), pp. 18–22. Condensed in *Education Digest,* II (May 1937), pp. 18–20.
46. "People's Choice," *High School Journal,* XXI (November 1938), pp. 247–252. Condensed in *Education Digest,* IV (January 1939), pp. 40–41.
47. "University's Responsibility in Adult Education," *Educational Method,* XVIII (March 1939), pp. 300–302.

48. "Effect of Community Forces upon the School," *National Education Association Journal*, XXVIII (April 1939), p. 101.

49. (Portrait), *School Executive*, LIX (September 1939), p. 32.

50. "Spirit of Democracy," *High School Journal*, XXII (December 1939), pp. 305–306.

51. "That Which Renders Men Incurious," *Childhood Education*, XVI (January 1940), p. 195.

52. "What Should Our Children Inherit?" *American Teacher*, XXIV (February 1940), pp. 10–11, 18–19. Condensed in *Education Digest*, V (April 1940), pp. 1–7.

53. (Portrait), *Nation's Schools*, XXV (March 1940), p. 39.

54. "Give Them All a Break," *Frontiers of Democracy*, VI (May 1940), pp. 246–247.

55. "Some Comments on the Administrator's Task," *Childhood Education*, XVII (September 1940), pp. 8–11.

56. (Portrait), *Arizona Teacher-Parent*, XXIX (November 1940), p. 15.

57. "With Liberty and Justice for All," *National Parent-Teacher*, XXXV (November 1940), pp. 7–9.

58. "Not What It Used to Be. . .And Never Was," *Frontiers of Democracy*, VII (December 1940), pp. 80–82.

59. "Adequate Public School Programs," pp. 40–46, in *Coordination of School and Community* (University of Pennsylvania School of Education 27th Annual Schoolmen's Meeting). Philadelphia: University of Pennsylvania School of Education, 1941.

60. "Problems of Pupil Adjustment in the Secondary School and Their Implications for the School Administrator," pp. 87–92, in *Coordination of School and Community* (University of Pennsylvania School of Education 27th Annual Schoolmen's Meeting). Philadelphia: University of Pennsylvania School of Education, 1941.

61. "School and College Re-Study Their Charters," pp. 32–38, in American College Personnel Association, *Report of the Eighteenth Annual Meeting*. Urbana: University of Illinois, 1941.

62. "Protecting our Educational Ideals: Defense Is Not by Guns Alone," *American Association of University Women Journal*, XXXIV (June 1941), pp. 211–216.

63. (With H. C. Hand), "This War and America: Objection," *Frontiers of Democracy*, VIII (October 1941), pp. 19–20.

64. "Paleolithic Defense," *School and Society*, LIV (Oct. 11, 1941), pp. 210–212.

65. "Better Relationships in the Western Hemisphere," *National Education Association Proceedings* (1941), pp. 45–50. Reprinted as "Better Relations with Latin America," *National Education Association Journal*, XXX, no. 7 (October 1941), pp. 203–204.

66. "Adult Education during the Sixty Years' War," *Journal of Adult Education*, XIII (October 1941), pp. 359–364.

67. "Interchange of Cultural Viewpoints," *Phi Delta Kappan*, XXIV (November 1941), pp. 101–103.

68. T. M. Carter, "J. Abner Peddiwell Speaks Again," *School and Society*, LIV (Nov. 22, 1941), pp. 471–472.

69. "America Must Be Strong, and Smart, Too, If Possible," *Pennsylvania School Journal*, XC (February 1942), pp. 204–206.

70. "War Measure for Adult Education, *Adult Education Bulletin*, VI (February 1942), p. 67.

71. (Portrait), *Kentucky School Journal*, XX (April 1942), p. 18.

72. "Soldier's Education for Peace," *Frontiers of Democracy*, VIII (April 1942), pp. 205–207.

73. "Progress in Education and Recreation," *Education for Victory*, I (June 1, 1942), pp. 26–28.

74. "Of Greater Moment Than Guns," *Educational Leadership*, I (October 1943), p. 1.

75. "Program for Military Personnel Commended by Educator," *School Management*, XV (September 1945), p. 28.

76. "New U.S. Office of Education Appointments," *School Executive*, LXV (December 1945), p. 38.

77. "After Taps Comes Reveille," *American Association of School Administrators Official Report* (1945–1946), pp. 103–108.

78. (With M. B. Lourenco), "Education," pp. 103–112, in *Handbook of Latin American Studies*. Cambridge, Mass.: Harvard University Press, 1946.

79. "New Positions and Appointments in U.S. Office of Education," *School Life*, XXVIII (February 1946), p. 7.

80. "Cultural Engineering," *Minnesota Journal of Education*, XXVI (May 1946), p. 375.

81. "Role of Education in the Twentieth Century Revolution," *Educational Forum*, X (May 1946), pp. 417–422.

82. "New Education for a New Japan," *School Life*, XXVIII (June 1946), pp. 1, 3–4.

83. "Higher Education in Japan," *Higher Education*, III (Sept. 2, 1946), pp. 5–7.

84. "UNESCO: Report from the United States," *School Life*, XXIX (October 1946), p. 9.

85. "Sarmiento the Educator," pp. 7–16, in University of Texas Institute of Latin American Studies No. 5, *Some Educational and Anthropological Aspects of Latin American Education*. Austin: The Institute, 1947.

86. "Responsibility of the School," *School Executive*, LXVI (January 1947), pp. 46–47.

87. "Developing and Maintaining the Morale of Teachers," pp. 54–58, in *Education in Transition* (University of Pennsylvania School of Education 34th Annual Schoolmen's Week Proceedings). Philadel-

phia: University of Pennsylvania School of Education, 1947. Reprinted in *Educational Outlook*, XXI (May 1947), pp. 149–152.

88. "Contribution of Education to World Security through Improved Communication," *North Central Association Quarterly*, XXII (October 1947), pp. 168–173.

89. "Our Golden Age Is Now," *Educational Leadership*, V (October 1947), pp. 3–6.

90. "Improved Communication for World Security," *Modern Language Journal*, XXXI (November 1947), pp. 409–415.

91. "Teachers Make the Schools," *Survey Graphic*, XXXVI (November 1947), pp. 624–626.

92. "Educational Design for the Great Society," *California Journal of Elementary Education*, XVI (November 1947), pp. 75–86. Condensed in *Education Digest*, XIV (October 1948), pp. 43–46.

93. "Ph.D.'s Preferred," *Journal of Higher Education*, XIX (April 1948), pp. 189–193.

94. "Place of the Secondary School in American Society," *School Review*, LVI (November 1948), pp. 510–518.

95. "The International Challenge to Teacher Education," *American Association of Colleges for Teacher Education* (Second Yearbook) (1949), pp. 117–122.

96. "Education in a Democracy," *Annals of the American Academy of Political and Social Science*, CCLXV (September 1949), pp. 10–16.

97. "Our People," *National Education Association Journal*, XXXVIII (October 1949), pp. 504–505.

98. (Portrait), *Phi Delta Kappan*, XXXI (November 1949), p. 147.

99. "Role of Higher Education in American Democracy," pp. 3–14, in *Democracy in the Administration of Higher Education* (Tenth Yearbook of the John Dewey Society). New York: Harper and Brothers, 1950.

100. "American Education in the Twentieth Century, Second Half," *American Association of Colleges for Teacher Education Yearbook* (1950), pp. 184–190.

101. "UNESCO's Educational Missions," *Harvard Educational Review*, XX, no. 3 (1950), pp. 228–232.

102. "Mission to Afghanistan," *Phi Delta Kappan*, XXXI (May 1950), pp. 442–445.

103. "Education Faces the World Crisis," *Educational Record*, XXXI (July 1950), pp. 283–292.

104. "Report on the Enemy," *Virginia Journal of Education*, XLIV (September 1950), pp. 23–24. Reprinted with commentary on pp. 137–143, in Ernest Oscar Melby and Morton Puner (eds.), *Freedom and Public Education*. New York: Frederick A. Praeger, Inc., 1953.

105. "Education's Role in the World Crisis," *Educational Leadership*, VIII (October 1950), pp. 4–6.

106. "The Curriculum and Social Education," pp. 23–28, in Eldridge Tracy McSwain and Jack R. Childress (comps. and eds.), *Opportuni-*

ties for Education in the Next Decade [Conference for Administrative Officers of Public and Private Schools Proceedings I (1951)]. Chicago: University of Chicago Press, 1951.

107. "Education to Preserve Democracy in Times of Conflict," pp. 73–90, in Charles Moore Allen and J. Lloyd Trump (eds.), Education during World Transition (Proceedings of the Conference). Urbana: University of Illinois Press, 1951.

108. "United Nations' Human Rights Program," Journal of Negro Education, XX, no. 3 (1951), pp. 256–260.

109. "On Magic Gadgets in Education," Peabody Journal of Education, XXVIII, no. 4 (January 1951), pp. 196–197.

110. We Develop Discipline for Freedom," Childhood Education, XXVII (January 1951), p. 199.

111. "Education Faces the World Crisis," The Peabody Reflector, XXIV, no. 2 (February 1951), pp. 36–39, 48.

112. "True Faith and Allegiance: An Inquiry into Education for Human Brotherhood and Understanding," National Education Association Journal, XL (February 1951), pp. 126–127.

113. "Direction of Elementary Education," National Elementary Principal, XXX (June 1951), p. 41.

114. "Quem di Perdere Volunt: poem," Peabody Journal of Education, XXIX (July 1951), p. 23.

115. "These Rights and Privileges," Commencement Address, June 8, 1951, The Peabody Reflector, XXIV, nos. 6 and 7 (June-July 1951), pp. 164–166.

116. (Column editor), "The Importance of People," Educational Leadership, IX, no. 1
(October 1951), pp. 45–48; IX, no. 2 (November 1951), pp. 125–127; IX, no. 3
(December 1951), pp. 189–191; IX, no. 4 (January 1952), pp. 243–245; IX, no. 5
(February 1952), pp. 317–320; IX, no. 6 (March 1952), pp. 383–385; IX, no. 7
(April 1952), pp. 449–451; IX, no. 8 (May 1952), pp. 519–521; X, no. 1
(October 1952), pp. 43–47; X, no. 2 (November 1952), pp. 119–122; X, no. 3
(December 1952), pp. 181–183; X, no. 4 (January 1953), pp. 253–257; X, no. 5
(February 1953), pp. 309–312; X, no. 7 (April 1953), pp. 445–449, 453

117. "Schools Should Teach the Fundamentals! Whose Fundamentals?" Phi Delta Kappan, XXXIII (October 1951), pp. 87–89. Condensed in Education Digest, XVII (December 1951), pp. 5–7.

118. "Changing Scenes," Peabody Journal of Education, XXIX, no. 3 (November 1951), pp. 143–144.

119. "Purposes in the Social Foundations of Education Division," The Peabody Reflector, XXIV, no. 10 (December 1951), pp. 285, 286.

120. "Conference Highlights: Second Day's Session," pp. 79–82, in

Francis H. Horn (ed.), *Current Issues in Higher Education* (National Conference on Higher Education Official Reports). Washington, D.C.: Association for Higher Education, 1952.

121. "Academic Manners of the Americans," *Peabody Journal of Education*, XXIX (January 1952), pp. 202–211.

122. "Education in Afghanistan," *Educational Outlook*, XXVI (January 1952), pp. 67–74.

123. "Education: What and How? A Debate," *Journal of Higher Education*, XXIII (January 1952), pp. 27–31.

124. "The Measurement of College Character," *The Peabody Reflector*, XXV, no. 2 (February 1952), pp. 32–33ff.

125. "New Subversion," *American Association of University Women Journal*, XLV (March 1952), pp. 151–153.

126. "Old Man Coyote and the 2nd Lieutenants," *The Peabody Reflector*, XXV, no. 3 (March 1952), pp. 55–57.

127. "Silver River and Golden Land," *Educational Outlook*, XXVI (March 1952), pp. 102–106.

128. "What Makes Schools Better?" *National Association of Secondary School Principals Bulletin*, XXXVI (April 1952), pp. 374–378.

129. "Challenge to Public Education," *College and University*, XXVII (July 1952), pp. 510–514.

130. "Communication Affecting Education," pp. 87–118, in *Forces Affecting American Education* (Association for Supervision and Curriculum Development Yearbook). Washington, D.C.: National Education Association, 1953.

131. "Cultures in Conflict," pp. 3–13, in *Great Human Issues of Our Time*. Nashville, Tenn.: Bureau of Publication, George Peabody College for Teachers, 1953.

132. "How Can We Achieve Adequate Public Understanding of Education?" pp. 8–12, in Raymond F. Howes (ed.), *Toward Unity in Educational Policy*. Washington, D.C.: American Council on Education, 1953.

133. "Foreign Languages in American Schools," *The Peabody Reflector*, XXVI, no. 2 (February 1953), pp. 29–30.

134. "Controversial Issues in American Life—Their Effect on the School Curriculum," *The Peabody Reflector*, XXVI, no. 3 (March 1953), p. 50.

135. "Where Are Our Schools Going? (Review of *Quackery in the Public Schools* by Albert Lynd)," *The Peabody Reflector*, XXVI, no. 9 (October 1953), pp. 191, 194.

136. "Languages in General Education," *Modern Language Journal*, XXXVII (November 1953), pp. 327–330. Condensed in *Education Digest*, XIX (February 1954), pp. 37–39.

137. "And Never Was," *Peabody Journal of Education*, XXXI, no. 5 (March 1954), pp. 260–261. Condensed in *Education Digest*, XX (September 1954), pp. 40–41.

138. "How Much for What," *Childhood Education*, XXXI (October 1954), p. 55.

139. "How Effectively Are We Teaching the Fundamentals?" pp. 33–39, in *Pennsylvania University Schoolmen's Week Proceedings*. Philadelphia: University of Pennyslvania School of Education, 1956.

140. "Growth in Comparative Education," *Phi Delta Kappan*, XXXVII (January 1956), pp. 141–144.

141. "Poverty of Nations," *Personnel and Guidance Journal*, XXXV (November 1956), pp. 140–144.

142. "Some Measures of Quality in Teacher Education," *Education Digest*, XXII (March 1957), pp. 29–31.

143. ". . .And With the Other Hand. . .A Weapon," *Educational Forum*, XXII (November 1957), pp. 5–12.

144. "Whom the Gods Destroy, They First Make Ludicrous," *Social Education*, XXII (February 1958), pp. 55–58.

145. "The Saber-Tooth Tiger Returns," *National Association of Secondary School Principals Bulletin*, XLII, no. 237 (April 1958), pp. 358–366.

146. "Education: Maker and Breaker of Nations," pp. 81–90, in American Association of School Administrators, *Official Report 1960*. Washington, D.C.: The Association, 1960. Reprinted in *The Peabody Reflector*, XXXIII, no. 2 (May-June 1960), pp. 38–39.

147. "The Problems of Education," pp. 373–388, in Lyman Bryson (ed.), *An Outline of Man's Knowledge of the Modern World*. New York: McGraw-Hill Book Company, 1960.

148. "The Curious Case of Homo the Non-Sapient and His Seven Smart Sons," *University of South Florida Educational Review*, II, no. 1 (Fall 1963), pp. 1–7.

149. "Higher Education in Latin America," *Phi Delta Kappan*, XLV, no. 4 (January 1964), pp. 178–182.

150. "Criteria for Judging the Worth of an International Educational Program," pp. 11–15, in Stewart E. Fraser (ed.), *Governmental Policy and International Education*. New York: John Wiley & Sons, Inc., 1965. 373 pp.

151. "To His Full Height: Commencement Address, August 20, 1966," *The Peabody Reflector*, XXXIX, no. 5 (September-October 1966), pp. 198–200.

152. Robert M. Bruker, "An Acquaintance of Yours: Harold R. W. Benjamin," *Peabody Journal of Education*, XLVI, no. 4 (January 1969), pp. 241–242.

153. "Latin America: Educational Perceptions," pp. 73–79, in Stewart E. Fraser (ed.), *International Education: Understandings and Misunderstandings*. Nashville, Tenn.: Peabody International Center, 1969. 79 pp. Reprinted in *The Peabody Reflector*, XLII, no. 1 (January-February 1969), pp. 11–14.

Obituaries

154. Baltimore *Sun*, Jan. 14, 1969.
155. Nashville *Banner*, Jan. 13, 1969, p. 2; Jan. 15, 1969, p. 7; Jan. 16, 1969, p. 51; and Jan. 18, 1969, p. 15.
156. Nashville *Tennessean*, Jan. 14, 1969, p. 7; Jan. 15, 1969, p. 12.
157. Washington, D.C., *Post*, Jan. 14, 1969.
158. New York *Times*, Jan. 14, 1969, p. 45.
159. Washington, D.C., *Evening Star*, Jan. 14, 1969, p. B-5.
160. Stanley Drazek, "Obituary," *Adult Leadership*, XVII (February 1969), p. 359.
161. Clifton L. Hall, "A Tribute to Harold Benjamin," *The Peabody Reflector*, XLII, no. 1 (January-February 1969), pp. 9–10.
162. [John E. Windrow], "Harold R. W. Benjamin 1893–1969," *The Peabody Reflector*, XLII, no. 1 (January-February 1969), pp. 2–8.
163. Franklin Parker, "In Memoriam: Harold R. W. Benjamin, 1893–1969," *Kappa Delta Pi Record*, V, no. 3 (February 1969), p. 93.
164. Arthur H. Moehlman, "Harold R. W. Benjamin — 1893–1969," *Southwestern Philosophy of Education Society Newsletter*, VI, no. 2 (March-April 1969), pp. 2–3.
165. "Obituary," *Educational Forum*, XXXIII (March 1969), p. 405.
166. William Van Til, "Three Good Men," *Contemporary Education*, XL (May 1969), pp. 369–370.
167. George J. Kabat, "In Memoriam: Harold R. W. Benjamin 1893–1969," *Educational Forum*, XXXIV, no. 4 (May 1970), pp. 505–512.
168. Clifton L. Hall, "Harold R. W. Benjamin Remembered," *Western Carolina University Journal of Education*, II, no. 2 (Fall 1970), pp. 34–36.

Unpublished Manuscripts and Speeches
(In Library of Congress, Washington, D.C.)

Unpublished manuscripts
169. "To Hell and Gone"
170. "The Trail of Medicine Dog"
Unpublished Speeches
171. "Protecting the Rights and Advancing the Responsibilities of the Teaching Profession," Address at the First National Workshop on Professional Rights and Responsibilities, National Education Association Convention, Denver, Colo., June 30, 1962.
172. "Old Man Coyote and His Crystal Ball," Address before the 4th Armed Forces Educational Conference, University of Maryland, Dec. 7, 1962.
173. "Riders to Set Upon Them" Senior Convocation Address, Glassboro State College, June 2, 1963

174. "Dimensions of Educational Policy," The Sarah Olive Rush Lecture delivered at the University of South Florida, Feb. 7, 1964.

175. "On the Practice of Magic in Education" and "Revolution by Education in the Twenty-first Century," the EDUCARE lectures at the University of Southern California, Spring 1965.

176. "Professional Drive: Its Nature and Nurture," Graduate School Convocation Address, Syracuse University, July 1, 1965.

177. "Some Revolutionary Advice from a Member of the Class of 1914," Commencement Address at Southern Illinois University, June 9, 1967.